Rotary Fly-Tying
Techniques

Understanding The Potential Of Your Rotary Fly-Tying Vise

Al & Gretchen Beatty

Rotary Fly-Tying
Techniques

Al & Gretchen Beatty

Frank Amato
PORTLAND

All inquiries should be addressed to:
Frank Amato Publications, Inc. • P.O. Box 82112 • Portland, Oregon 97282
503-653-8108 • www.amatobooks.com

"True Rotary" is a Registered Trademark of Renzetti, Inc. #75/519,221
Photography: Al & Gretchen Beatty
Book Design: Ann Amato/Mariah Hinds
Cover Design: Mariah Hinds
ISBN-13: 978-1-57188-418-3
UPC: 0-81127-00252-8
Printed in Hong Kong

1 3 5 7 9 10 8 6 4 2

Contents

Foreword

This book, *Rotary Fly-Tying Techniques*, is the first of its kind and long overdue, however rotary vises and some of the techniques are not necessarily new. At the 1991 Federation of Flyfishers Conclave I watched Sig Barnes tie a Goofus Bug on a treadle sewing machine converted into a fly-tying vise. Many years ago Dub Evans taught his daughter Gretchen (Beatty) to tie flies on a similar machine. In fact a number of people in the early days of fly tying used sewing machines to produce flies for our sport. Were they sewing machines, or rotary vises? My answer would be both, because while their intended use was a sewing machine they were modified to be the first true rotary v i s e s.

Like many fly tiers I started on a Thompson A vise. Eventually I graduated to a Regal vise. As Al explains it in this book, the Regal is a full-rotation vise, not a true rotary vise. I tied on this vise for many years and used it for all my commercial tying. One of the features I liked about it was that I would rest my left hand on the vise and turn it from side to side as I was tying the fly. This rocking motion allowed me a better view of the fly as it was being constructed. Today there are thousands of rotary vises in the hands of fly tiers. These tiers have a varied level of skills ranging from novice to professional. It is my opinion that the majority of these tiers use their true rotary vises for the same purpose I did, or worse yet, use the vise for only one purpose, holding the hook. Unfortunately most tiers do not fully grasp the potential of their true rotary vise.

In 1999 Al presented me with a Danvise, which is a true rotary vise, and one of his rotary tying videos. Very honestly, before he gave me the vise and before I watched the video I never gave much credence to rotary vises or the methods and ways to use them. Today I never teach a class or demonstrate fly tying at a show without using some rotary techniques. The reason is simple; the word has to get out.

Al Beatty and I have worked, fished, and tied flies together for a good many years. I know him well. One word to describe him is intense. He is a tremendous innovator and fly tier. He puts the same energy into his writing, and with Gretchen's editing skills the words from this team flow on the page. I assure you this book, *Rotary Fly-Tying Techniques*, is certainly no exception. They did not just sit down and write/edit a book. It is an accumulation of years of experimentation and tying with rotary vises.

Rotary Fly-Tying Techniques has three basic focal points. One is a sampling of various true rotary vises available on the market today. The next point is fly patterns, and the most important aspect of the book is the actual rotary tying techniques. As I stated earlier Al is an innovator, he actually is a master at this. It will amaze you the simple techniques that are outlined here which will aid you in the construction of flies. Ease and speed of construction are points that will be learned. In addition, *Rotary Fly-Tying Techniques* will teach you how to construct stronger, better-looking flies.

As a friend it is very easy for me to say this, but we should all be thankful for the efforts put forth by the team (Al and Gretchen Beatty) in writing this book and sharing their knowledge with us.

—*Bob Lay*
Helena, Montana

About This Book

In the past our readers have come to understand a reference to the authors was accomplished using the word "we," plural for the singular "I." That word always worked well for us because we were working from a common base of experience explaining how a certain fly pattern or technique was accomplished. Yes, Al wrote most of the first draft on any project and Gretchen polished his words into a final version. That approach really worked well for us as long as we were dealing with a subject in which we shared fairly equal skills.

Our second book *Tying Hair Wing Flies* fits very well into this scenario. At the time we completed it we were tying commercially a couple thousand-dozen hair-wing flies a year. The book was nothing more than many hours at the vise cooked down into several chapters explaining a winter's work. We often spent several weeks tying the same fly, same size, same materials, using the same techniques. If one of us stumbled onto a technique that would improve our productivity or quality we shared it with the other person. Then it was back to the same fly, size, materials, etc. using the new technique. Writing about something we both accomplished using almost identical movements was really quite easy. Then this book came along. Our skills regarding rotary tying have very different backgrounds and skill levels. Let us explain.

Gretchen learned to tie from her father William J. "Dub" Evans on a treadle sewing machine he had converted into a rotary vise. She started at the age of six sitting beside him sorting his materials while he tied commercial orders on his treadle vise. When she was tall enough to reach the treadle she could be found at the vise trying her hand at tying while he worked at his regular day job as a plumbing/heating contractor. Their tools were simple. The vise, scissors, fingers, and feet (operating the treadle) were all that a tier needed to render a stack of materials into an order of flies going out the door to a customer. Imagine Gretchen's dismay when she sat down with Al to produce their first commercial order together. Her first comment to him was, "What are all these tools?" At this point let's put this story on hold for a moment and take a look at Al's fly-tying background.

Al started tying flies after receiving a Herter's fly-tying kit for his fourteenth birthday. It contained an inexpensive vise and an assortment of tools (bobbin, scissors, hackle pliers, stacker, etc.). He didn't have a fly rod yet and soon figured out he could sell flies to earn the money to make this purchase. After a year of tying for a local hardware store and trapping pocket gophers for the bounty he made the grand purchase of a fly rod, automatic reel, and a level line. He was ready to go fly-fishing! Along the path to earning his new fly rod Al figured out he could make money tying flies and has been a commercial tier ever since.

It wasn't long and Al upgraded his original vise to a Thompson B, then along came a Thompson A, and finally the best of the best, an original HMH rotating vise. The HMH gave him the ability to look at the other side of the fly and also reposition the pattern so he could complete some tasks easier. Al didn't have the HMH long before he figured out he could reposition the jaw parallel with the tying table and rotate the vise to speed up some tying functions. The increased speed was great but the hook shank bouncing up and down because it was not on axis proved to be a real pain in the neck. Not long after this discovery he stumbled on an old Universal rotary vise in an antique store and really discovered the pleasure of true rotary tying. The years slid by and more true rotary vises found their way into Al's tying room. Yes, he still loved to tie on the old HMH rotating vise but the true rotary vises had found a special place in his heart.

As often happens in a business, it evolves, and it was no different for Al's commercial tying enterprise. In time most of his orders were for hair-wing dry flies and the rotating style of vise like the HMH really worked best. It was particularly great for repositioning a Humpy or Wulff to get an even division on the two clumps of hair in the wings. The true rotary vises just didn't work as well for this function and found themselves relegated to a storage box.

Through this whole timeline Gretchen had put her tying on hold in the interest of raising a family and pursuing a career. Her business skills eventually led her to GTE (now called Verizon) as a human resource manager where she met Al whose day job was a management position in field operations. In time she learned about his night job as a commercial tier and their common interest developed into a friendship. Over the next ten years that friendship grew into something more and the two were married in 1993. To that marriage Al brought a flourishing fly-tying business and Gretchen brought an old treadle fly-tying machine constructed by her father. Their early months together were spent teaching Gretchen how to tie hair-wing flies on an HMH vise so she could help Al with the increasing demand for those patterns. His true rotary vises stayed in a box and hers went into storage in the garage.

Shortly after their wedding the two retired from GTE and moved to Montana to write, tie, and guide. During the next years the couple were inseparable whether at the vise, on the stream, or at the keyboard.

During their Montana years, Johnny Fisker from Denmark asked the couple to distribute his true-rotary Danvise in the United States and they agreed. Al reached back in his memory bank and brought his dusty rotary-tying skills out of storage. Soon those skills were again finely tuned and as he became more familiar with the Danvise his dexterity grew as well. The couple produced their video "Rotary Tying Techniques" to enhance the sales potential of the vise and it proved quite successful.

Al and Gretchen continue tying commercially, Al on the Danvise and Gretchen on a Griffin's Patriot she has learned to love. When the two decided to write this book they found themselves in a new position; neither was an expert in the complete subject. Gretchen was very skilled in rotary tying on a treadle-driven machine while Al was unable to even get thread on the hook with "that backwards thing!" On the other hand, Gretchen was much more skilled in the use of a rotating vise, like the Griffin's Patriot, while Al was much more comfortable with the true rotary Danvise. The couple decided to switch from the word "we" indicating an equal knowledge basis and start using the word "I." In so doing they switched roles depending on the subject. Gretchen writes about the history and the treadle machine while Al does the editing. Al does the writing when talking about modern-day, true-rotary vises and Gretchen does the editing. When you see the word "I" you may not know which one of the team did the editing or the writing but rest assured they have one goal in mind: to make the topic as clear as possible for you the reader.

With that thought in mind, we want to welcome all of you to *Rotary Fly-Tying Techniques*. We have some history and a bunch of tying tricks to share with you. Let's get started!

—*Al & Gretchen Beatty*
Boise, Idaho

Introduction

Several years ago I attended the San Mateo, California International Sportsmen's Exposition to operate a BT's Fly Fishing Products booth and participate in the Video Fly Tying Theater. The theater is in a room at the end of a long hall. This hall has about ten fly tiers stationed along one side to provide instruction for the audience unable to get a seat in the theater. I had a few minutes before my scheduled program so I decided to watch the tiers on station in the hall. Interestingly all of them were using a true rotary unit of one design or another, all vises above what I would call the mid-price range. None of the tiers used their vise for anything more than to occasionally look at the other side of the fly. By the way, those vises did that function very well, but to my way of thinking the dollars involved made looking at the other side of the fly a pretty expensive proposition.

Right there in the hall I decided to change my program to Rotary Tying Techniques and show the audience what they could expect from a true rotary vise. Since that time I've done that program in one form or another many, many times all over the world. This year when I participated in that same video theater I again had a few minutes to observe before my program. Seven of the ten tiers were using a true rotary vise and six of them were using the rotation feature to apply materials to the hook.

Did my presentation several years earlier and those subsequent programs make a difference? Who knows! I sure would like to think it did. Hopefully this book will also help you fly tiers using true rotary vises unlock the potential within. I'm confident the tips and tricks in these pages will have something for tiers at all skill levels.

Interestingly in looking at the history of the rotary vise I found Gretchen's family to be involved at the very beginning of the true rotary revolution in regard to its use in the commercial fly-tying world in the early years of the 20th century. I'll talk about that more in the historical section. After looking at the history and constructing a couple flies using old-style vises, I think a comparison between a true rotary vise and a full-rotation vise is in order. In the next chapters you'll discover what you must un-learn in order to successfully put a true rotary vise through its paces. With this un-learning process behind us, you and I will have completed the introductory part of the book. Then we can really have some fun as we move into the body of the book.

The rest of the story is a review of twenty-five or so techniques employed on flies that best illustrate my message. Each chapter will feature a vise by a different manufacturer, a little history of the tool/company, and several flies that effectively demonstrate the equipment and at least one technique. One of the chapters will feature a prototype vise developed by Jeff Smith and me with features never before seen. It will do things no other vise can but more on that later. Now let's take a look at the history of the true rotary vise OR at least what I was able to find in that regard.

A Glance at History

It is not my purpose in writing this book to present a completely researched history of the true rotary vise. Rather these pages are intended to introduce the reader to rotary, fly-tying techniques that can help a tier achieve speed, dexterity, and consistency never before realized using a standard vise.

However, I do believe a book on the subject would be less than complete if it did not review at least some of the history. Besides, Gretchen would kill me if I didn't mention her family was quite involved in the commercial fly-tying business using treadle sewing machines converted into rotary vises. It all started with Gretchen's Aunt Lois Coon who tied part-time for the Glen L. Evans Company from 1935 to about 1940. In 1945 shortly after World War II, Gretchen's father William J. "Dub" Evans built his first rotary vise out of a Singer treadle machine and plumbing parts; he worked as a plumber in his day job so they were readily available. His wife Catherine suggested he design his machine so it was similar to the one her sister Lois tied on at the fly factory, which he did matching it as closely as possible considering the crude materials. Dub cut the sewing machine in half and poured it full of lead to act as a bearing for the rotating part of the vise. The jaws pointed to the left so the spool/spindle would line up with the wheel on the treadle mechanism. He also cut the treadle in half and attached an arm to each piece so the tier would not hit "dead center" and have to hand start the machine. Using this treadle vise he started a part-time, commercial fly-tying operation.

His fly-tying business eventually grew to the point he needed help. Dub built two more rotary vises and hired his sister-in-law and another lady to tie for him. The later two machines had bicycle front-wheel axles for the

The jaws were constructed from plumbing materials.

rotating part welded to the jaw assembly constructed from plumbing parts. In time Dub's plumbing business grew to the point he no longer had the time to continue tying flies on a commercial basis. He retired the vise to using it only a few times a year to supply flies for his own fishing. Today it is on display at the Federation of Fly Fishers Museum in Livingston, Montana. Gretchen ended up with one of the other two and unfortunately a relative took the third machine to the dump not knowing what it was.

For years Gretchen's machine was stored in the garage. When we started this book I decided to refurbish it to photograph her father tying a fly. Naturally Gretchen decided to test drive her old friend and completed a fly

Even though he used a walker to reach the machine, "Dub" Evans could still spin his magic at ninety years young.

with relative ease. Not to be outdone I sat down to have a go at tying with my feet/hands. That was a couple of months ago and I've still not finished a complete fly. Often it is a struggle just to get a thread base on the hook. What a role reversal! I've always been the expert and now the tables have turned. Some of you are probably chuckling at me about now, but I'd sure like to see you put thread on a left-handed hook with your feet!

Gretchen tells us in her own words about tying on the vise. She'll have to explain it to all of you: When I was younger, I never could understand why anyone would tie on a stationary vise. Watching my father tie with the snelled hook rotating at his bidding was the only thing that made sense to me. How slow and difficult I thought it must be to wind the thread and the material around the hook by 'hand'. Watching the hackle flare around the hook as the jaws rotated was pure magic and I knew from a very young age that I wanted to do that...someone else could read or cook or sew, I was going to tie flies.

The treadle vise I tied on was converted by my father, William J. Evans, and was based loosely on the machines used in Glen L. Evans's factory. The jaws were made from plumbing parts and were designed to open and close when you rotated the vise. This arrangement, although far different from the midge jaws available today, served our needs well as we did not tie on hooks much smaller than a size 12 or 14.

The machines were designed with the clamp or vise coming from the right hand side. As a result I learned how to do everything backwards from a regular right-handed tier. For example, I did the finger thumb tuck with the right hand when I set quill wings; I held them with my right hand and used my left to pull the thread tight. Al not only had to introduce me to the tools and tying thread (we used sewing thread), I had to relearn a lot of moves. Even today when I am setting up to demonstrate, I have to pause as I am clamping the vise to the table to ensure I have it facing the right direction. Perhaps I should try tying left-handed. It would be handy as an instructional tool.

Before anyone can be successful tying on a converted treadle sewing machine, they must learn to control the rotation of the vise, stop and start it, and apply a base thread wrap. At first it can be very frustrating when you try to go forward and end up removing the previous material because you are going backwards. The machines were not all the same. Some of the treadles were split and some were a single platform. I found on the machine I used, a single-platform treadle, that the placement of my feet was very important; my right foot needed to be further forward than the left. A push by the toes of the right foot would start the forward motion. A push by the heel of my left foot would start a backward rotation. I stopped and held the rotation still by centering both feet and applying a constant pressure with the heels of each. Some tiers pressed their knee to the wheel to stop the motion, but I was too short to do that effectively.

There are several different techniques we used to tie on that treadle

Gretchen takes her old friend
for a test drive.

One of the machines from the Glen L. Evans Company courtesy of Howard's Fly Shop & Back Room Bargains in Nampa, Idaho.

machine. First of all it was essential for me to have all of the materials sized and laid out before I began to tie. Since we did not use a bobbin there was no weight to hold the thread in place. A long piece of thread was cut from the spool, attached to the hook and kept taut either by holding it in your hand or by wrapping it around a nail or hook pounded into the edge of the tying surface. Wrapping it around the nail to free your hands to sort materials was just too time-consuming so preparation was an efficiency issue. Dad used lead printers' rectangles to hold the material in a neat pile ready for use. In later years, I used baby food jar lids. Tiers will always improvise.

Another little trick on these machines, and for that matter in all rotary tying, is to lead with the thread and follow with the material. This keeps the thread from ruining the material as it wraps over it. With practice, you can hold both the thread and the material with one hand while rotating the machine and reaching for the next material with your free hand. After some additional experience, you can apply several different materials at a time. For example, when tying a Woolly Bugger you can wrap the thread, chenille, and hackle forward all at once. This is how you really begin to cut the minutes from your tying time.

Next is how to do an easy, quick whip finish. You simply make a loop with the thread, take one wrap with the side of the loop made by the loose end, and rotate the vise holding that side so it wraps over the loop ends. After several wraps, pull the loose end of thread so the loop catches the eye.

Leaving Gretchen's reflections using the vise there are many more tips and techniques involved in rotary tying. The majority of these methods, however, applies to most rotary vises and will be covered throughout the book.

Before we leave the treadle machine part of our history I want to share a couple of tidbits about The Evans Fish Fly Company. First my father-in-law was not related to Glen, they just shared the same last name.

Chapter 1: A Glance at History

In 1922 the company was originally located on Main Street in Caldwell, Idaho but several years later Evans moved his company to Aven Street as part of an expansion. Over the years the company expanded six times as the organization evolved from a fly factory to a facility that manufactured all disciplines of fishing tackle, including rods wrapped on the treadle machines. Over time the name changed as well and when the company was sold to the Gladding Corporation it was the Glen L. Evans Company.

Long-time Treasure Valley resident and former fly-shop owner Ken Magee remembers the Dean Pollard vise first on the market in the mid 1970s.

John Joy, a Caldwell machinist, manufactured the first vises for Evans. His wife Audrey tied for the Evans Fish Fly Company for a number of years. After they moved to Portland, Oregon she tied in the fishing department at Meier & Frank. Audrey also demonstrated at fishing shows in the area and eventually became so popular she was selling her flies in five foreign countries, as well as here in the USA.

As near I can tell the Universal Vise was the first manually-operated consumer rotary vise. I've had a difficult time though identifying just when it was first available. In conversation with Mary Dette Clark from Roscoe, New York she seemed to remember tying on one in the late 30s. Steve Corey from 4-Corners Rod & Gun Shop in Columbia, Maine worked for Universal in the mid 70s. He remembers they had a brass version of the rotary vise on display at the plant dating back to the 50s. No matter when it was first available, rising production costs eventually

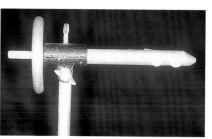

I think the Universal was the first consumer rotary vise. Some people argue it was not true rotary but I found that it was based on how the hook was mounted in the jaws.

drove it from the market in the mid 70s. For several years the company sold the Universal II a less expensive version but it too went by the wayside. I expect after these words are published someone will come forward with information about an earlier vise than the Universal. I sure hope so. It seems odd to me that creative minds developed a treadle vise for commercial work so long before a hand version was available to the general tying public.

In this brief look at history I do want to include what little information we have on the Electric Fly-Tying Vise manufactured by the Pollard Enterprises Company in Boise, Idaho. Long-time Treasure Valley resident and former fly-shop owner Ken Magee told me he thought Dean Pollard started manufacturing it in 70s.

He wasn't sure when he stopped production but I found an advertisement on page 23 in the 1984 Fall Issue of *The FlyFisher* magazine. That tells me it was manufactured at least until the mid 80s, but we have not been able to identify Mr. Pollard's status to learn more about the company or the vise. The tool itself is rather unique as you can see in the photograph. The jaws are split evenly from two directions allowing the hook positioning to fall on axis unlike some of the earlier treadle vises. The square red button starts and stops the rotation and the larger silver knob/ rheostat to the left adjusts the speed the hook turns. The large brown wheel on the end of the vise "kick starts" the rotation if the rheostat is adjusted too low.

Gretchen and I want to thank Howard Davis and Dennis Udlinek from Howard's Fly Shop & Back Room Bargains in Nampa, Idaho for loaning us the vise you see here. It's really kind of interesting how Howard ended up with the tool. Several years ago a local automobile mechanic accepted the vise in trade for work on a vehicle. The mechanic in turn traded the vise to Howard for fly-fishing supplies. The mechanic did not know the name of the person with whom he traded automobile work for the vise. If any of you reading this book have any information on Dean Pollard or his company, please email us at albeatty2@aol.com.

In 1979 Andy Renzetti introduced the bent-shaft style rotating arm revolutionizing the direction true rotary vises would take over the next twenty years. Almost all true rotary vises on the market today (except for a couple of exceptions like the Nor-Vise) hold the jaws at an angle similar to the Renzetti bent-arm design. The unit holding the jaws may look different but its purpose is to hold the hook on axis. This unit is our topic of discussion in the next chapter. Why? Because we must learn several techniques to work with the device so we may enjoy the many advantages a true rotary vise brings to the fly tier.

Relearning

Please read this chapter very carefully. I can't tell you the number of discouraged fly tiers I've communicated with who were frustrated with a recently purchased true-rotary vise. Their angst comes from trying to use skills designed for another vise style. Chances are

Fig. 1. An angle near ninety degrees produces a tightly spaced rib.

good that the true-rotary tool is an upgrade from a first vise like a Thompson "A" or something similar. The first time tying on the new unit often is an exercise in frustration because the tier's hand just doesn't fit like it used to. Nothing seems to work the same. In this short chapter I'll unlock the secrets to instant success with your great new purchase. All of my discussions in these pages are directed at the right-handed tier. If you are a lefty then reverse what I suggest.

The mechanism that allows the jaws on a true-rotary vise to hold a hook "on axis" is both wonderful and terrible at the same time. It's wonderful because it opens up a world of consistent material application difficult with a stationary vise. An evenly spaced rib on a fly is "a piece of cake" when using the rotating feature; the left hand rotates the vise while the right hand holds the material stationary. The angle the tier's right hand

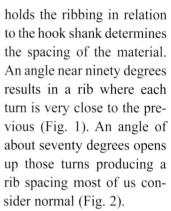

holds the ribbing in relation to the hook shank determines the spacing of the material. An angle near ninety degrees results in a rib where each turn is very close to the previous (Fig. 1). An angle of about seventy degrees opens up those turns producing a rib spacing most of us consider normal (Fig. 2).

This very same mechanism is also the source of frustration because it blocks the left hand from accessing the hook in the way most familiar. Let's tie a piece of material on several hooks first using an old Thompson

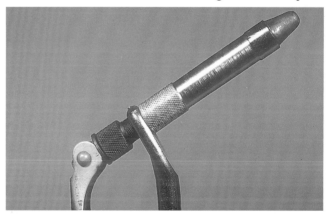

Fig. 3. The Thompson "A" vise is familiar to many fly tiers.

Fig. 2. A seventy-degree angle results in a more normal looking rib.

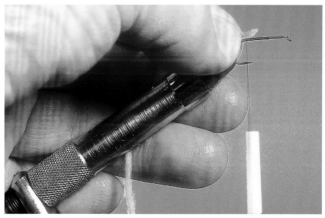

Fig. 4. There is plenty of room to allow access to the rear of the hook.

"A" vise I'vehad for many years and then using a true-rotary Danvise. As you'll see I have to employ different techniques to accomplish the same task based on the vise's design.

In the illustration (Fig 3) notice the Thompson vise's jaw points up at an angle of about forty-five degrees. There are no obstructions so the tier's hand can rest on the vise thus allowing access to the hook from rear (Fig. 4). The joint where my little finger joins the palm is the part of my hand resting on the vise. That's how many of us (me included) learned to tie tails/materials/stuff on a hook.

Now let's take a look at the Danvise (Fig. 5). Its jaw also is positioned at a forty-five-degree angle but the area directly behind it has an obstruction. I no longer have access to the hook from the rear like I did with my old Thompson vise. In fact if I rest my hand so it is at the same angle (aligned with the little finger/palm joint as in Fig. 4) the material between my thumb and forefinger is several inches above the vise (Fig. 6). Alas, a familiar tying technique just went flying out the window along with a splash of cold water in the face. After purchasing my first true-rotary vise I made this discovery on the very first fly and it took me the better part of a month to figure out what I'll share with you in the next paragraphs. Before continuing please understand I'm using the Danvise to illustrate this point because it's the tool I use on a daily basis. Don't think you will escape the dilemma because a different manufacturer produced your tool. Most true-rotary vises present the same problem to the tier so read on.

I offer three maneuvers that compensate for the obstruction behind the jaws. The first (Fig. 7) I call the tilt-and-angle method. The tier simply drops the fingers

Fig. 5. The true-rotary Danvise jaw is positioned at an angle similar to the Thompson "A" vise.

Fig. 6. When using familiar hand positioning on a true-rotary vise the material is several inches above the hook.

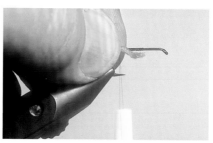

Fig. 7 The tilt-and-angle method places the material on the near side of the hook.

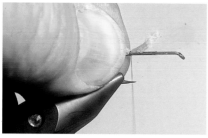

Fig. 8. Thread torque repositions the material from the side of the hook to the top of the shank.

Fig. 9. Start the offside method by positioning the hand on the vise at the junction of the wrist and the palm.

Fig. 10. The material is introduced to the hook at an angle across the top of the shank.

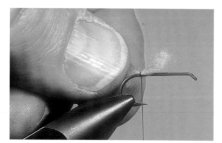

Fig. 11. Thread torque is employed to bring the material in line with the shank.

Fig. 12. Start the nearside method by resting the fingertips on the vise so the thumb and forefinger can access the hook.

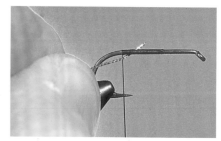

Fig. 13. Tying rib material to the underside of the hook.

holding the yarn down to meet the hook placing the material on the near side of it at an angle then using thread torque (Fig. 8) to reposition it to the top of the shank. I find this method works fairly well on larger hooks, but when I'm tying a tail on a size twenty or smaller it is not the solution for me. In that situation I've learned to reposition my hand so I can take advantage of the unobstructed *sides* of the vise.

I call the next two maneuvers off-side and nearside hand placement. My favorite is the offside method. To accomplish it I slide my hand away from me so the joint between the wrist and palm is resting on the vise rather than the junction between the palm and little finger (Fig. 9). When I tilt the fingers, holding the material down to meet the hook (Fig. 10) it is angled across the top of the shank from the offside. Now I use thread torque to position the strand of

Fig. 14. A feather can be easily attached to the bottom of the shank.

yarn/material (Fig. 11) in line with the shank.

The nearside hand placement maneuver is accomplished by resting the left hand (Fig. 12) on the vise by the fingertips allowing me to access that side of the hook. I don't particularly like this method for tying on tailing fibers, but it is great for anchoring ribbing material (Fig. 13) or a hackle feather (Fig. 14) to the underside of the hook.

There you have it, three very simple techniques to make tying flies on a true-rotary vise a pleasure instead of a problem. Take time to master each technique then enjoy learning the great potential stored in this really neat tool. I bet you thought the answer was much more complicated and of course that is not the case at all. Now let's have a little fun tying flies on three antique vises in the next chapter before moving on to their modern-day contemporaries reviewed in subsequent pages.

Tying on Antique Vises

I've really been looking forward to working on this chapter in which the patterns will be tied using the three antique vises we have. In some instances they require different techniques to dress a fly than do their modern counterparts. Like a lot of things in fly-tying though, the methods were developed many years ago. If a person thinks they have invented anything or developed a new pattern they really should take a hard look at history. It seems to me the only things that have really changed are new materials and the techniques required to work with them. One such method/material combination is Gary LaFontaine's use of Antron yarn to form a bubble around a caddis pupa body. That seems to me to be a new innovation while changing the color of a body or using a different material for an Adams dry fly falls short of the mark.

Enough of my ideas though, we're here to tie flies

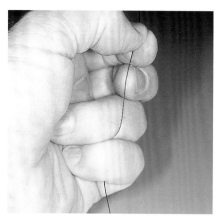

The thread is anchored in the crook of the left little finger.

on these old machines and I think "Woolly" style flies might be a fun way to begin tying rotary. Let's start with a standard Woolly Worm tied on Gretchen's treadle machine.

Before we actually start tying this simple but effective fly we need to talk about something many of us take for granted. In our day-to-day tying the weight of the bobbin is used to hold the thread in position and stop it from unwrapping. In the days commercial tiers dressed flies on treadle machines they did not use bobbins, instead they anchored the thread in the "crook" of their left, little finger like I am doing here. After anchoring the thread in this manner I can use the rest of my fingers to ready materials like preparing a hackle feather. I will be using this old-time technique through out the fly's construction. When you see the tying thread under tension and my left hand is out of the picture you will know what's happening.

Woolly Worm - Treadle

The Woolly Worm was a "first fly" for many tiers and I'm no exception. I guess it's appropriate that it should be my first fly on the treadle machine just like it was when I started tying flies in the late 1950s. I know I didn't struggle as much with that first Woolly Worm as I did with the treadle worm but I suppose time has a way of making one forget. Anyway enough of my troubles with the machine!

It still amazes me how many fish the pattern catches for me. It has spanned the ages and is as much a part of my fishing now that I'm in my sixties as it was in my

teens. I vividly remember a great brown trout I caught in the Madison River in the late 70s on a black Woolly Worm or the beautiful eleven-inch bluegill I landed last summer on an un-namedz pond in Oregon. My fly box always contains a fairly good selection of Woolly Worms and its cousin the Woolly Bugger. There is something irresistible about it to fish. I've never asked one what they liked about the Worm but I suspect it's the creepy/crawly ballet it performs under the waters' surface. Whatever the attraction let's now focus on tying it using a machine built in the 1940s.

Woolly Worm

Hook:	Size 2 to 16, streamer or wet style
Thread:	Black or matching color
Tail:	Bright yarn or hackle fibers
Hackle:	Grizzly or color of choice
Body:	Chenille, color of choice
Head:	Thread

Step 1: Just like tying any fly in a modern-day vise, start by placing the hook in the jaws. If you plan on pinching the barb do so before tying the fly. It's better to accidentally break the hook now, before investing the time tying the fly, than after. Select a three-foot section of un-waxed sewing thread and cut it from the spool. Strip it through a clump of bee's wax if you prefer this type of coating on your thread.

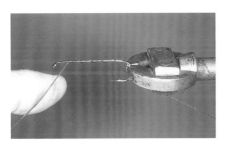

Step 2: I start the thread base at the back of the hook by placing the long end in my right hand and position it to the right of the jaws. Then use the left hand to wrap about five open turns of thread starting at the end of the shank and winding towards the hook eye.

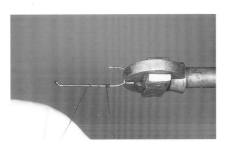

Step 3: Now I bring my right hand around so the thread it is holding forms a ninety-degree angle with the back of the hook shank. Holding my left hand slightly forward of the hook eye I use my feet to rotate the vise in the opposite direction that I wrapped the thread with my left hand. The spinning vise jaws start to apply the thread base while removing the original five left-hand turns.

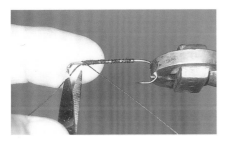

Step 4: As the last of those original turns are removed hold the segment of thread in the left hand straight out in front of the hook eye as the thread base moves forward on the shank. When I am very near the hook eye stop wrapping the thread and trim the end in my left hand. Note how I use the left trigger finger to keep the thread base from unwinding while making this cut.

Step 5: Wind the thread to the back of the hook. Cut a several-inch section of yarn (I used orange) for the tail. Tie it to the back of the shank with a couple of hand-wrapped thread turns. I then use my feet to spin the hook while holding the loose end of the yarn along the shank with my left hand. My right hand moves along the shank towards the eye binding the yarn to the hook. Stop near the eye, trim the waste end, and wind the thread to the back of the hook (remember, I'm turning the hook to accomplish this). Tie on a section of chenille and a grizzly hackle feather by the tip. Trim any waste ends.

Step 6: To this point I've only been wrapping thread over a hook or material. Now I'm going to advance material AND the thread together. There are only a few rules to tying flies by rotating the vise but there is one you may want to note. Let's call it Rule #1 of Rotary Fly-Tying (and probably the only rule). Whenever advancing thread with one or more materials it always leads the process. I'll probably mention that again several times as we progress through these pages. Using this rule I'll advance the chenille, the hackle, and the thread all at the same time, forming the rest of the fly in one step. My right hand holds the materials, the left is grasping the thread, and my feet are turning the vise. Notice my left trigger finger is controlling the chenille/hackle to keep them from running in front of the thread.

Step 7: Once I reach the front of the hook I'll take one turn of thread around the hackle and chenille. Now I pull the hackle out of my way and wrap two more turns of thread around the chenille and cut it from the hook. I'll not cut the hackle from the hook yet.

Step 8: Now I'll apply two more turns of hackle in front of the trimmed chenille. Next I tie it off and trim away the waste end. You'll note when tying rotary it seldom makes any difference where the hook point is as long as the material ends up in the proper place.

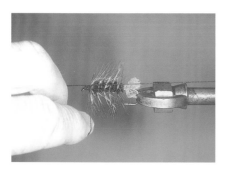

Step 9: While holding the tying thread taut I form the whip-finish triangle with the first and second finger of my left hand. Next I place this triangle next to the hook eye and rotate the vise jaws with my feet to apply the whip finish.

Step 10: Last I'll pull the whip-finish tight and trim off the waste end of thread. Putting a dab of Aqua Head on the whip-finish is really simple when turning the fly during the process. Note: Even though this appears near the front of the book I really wrote it near the end. It took me the better part of a year to learn to tie even the simplest of flies. I sure have a lot of respect for the people in history who tied thousands of dozen of flies on the treadle machines. My lovely wife Gretchen is at the top of the list.

Hot-Spot Woolly Bugger - Pollard Electric Vise

I do consider the Pollard Electric Fly-Tying Vise to be a part of history however it certainly is from the more recent past than a much older treadle machine. Therefore I don't feel too out of place using a bobbin to help construct this Woolly Bugger. While working with this vise I found I could use the little finger of my left hand to activate or stop the machine by simply adjusting the amount of pressure on the red button. In so doing I had the remaining fingers of my left hand to hold materials while the vise rotated the hook. Thankfully the jaws always turned in the same direction. I didn't have to put up with the same problem I encountered with the treadle vise; accidentally removing materials I had just applied to the hook. When I tied the Woolly Worm I had to redo it twice because I got the vise going in the wrong direction when trying to apply the whip-finish and lost everything. Believe me, tying on the Pollard vise was much easier.

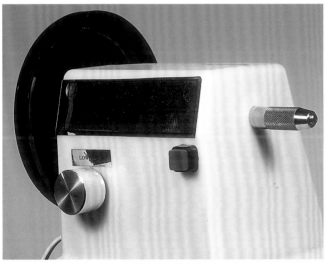

The Pollard Electric Fly Tying Vise is a more recent part of rotary tying history.

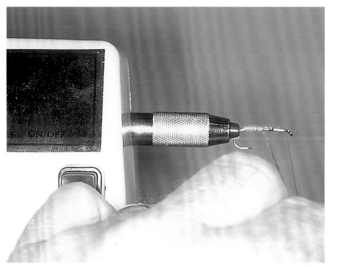

With a little practice I found using the knuckle of the left little finger to control the off/on switch of the vise while applying the materials with the other fingers worked best for me.

Hot-Spot Woolly Bugger

Hook:	Size 2 to 16, streamer or wet style
Thread:	Hot color of choice
Tail:	Marabou, color of choice
Hackle:	Brown or color of choice
Body:	Marabou, color of choice
Hot spot:	Thread, tag & head
Head:	Optional bead head

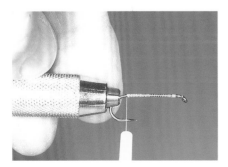

Step 1: Place the hook in the vise after pinching down the barb if releasing fish is your end-game plan. Lay down the thread base from just behind the hook eye to the end of the shank. I found I could really speed up the process by turning the vise while hand wrapping the thread at the same time. Note: The red button stops and starts the vise while the larger silver knob is used to adjust the rotation speed. I found the vise much easier to manage using a medium to slow rotation speed. The faster speeds really put material on the hook but it was also easy to lose control.

Step 2: Select a marabou feather (color of choice) and strip the short, fuzzy fibers from the base of the stem. Tie it to the end of the hook to form a tail that is about as long as the shank. Bind it to the hook forming a thread covering equal to about one-eighth inch. Be sure this thread application covers the marabou well as this is the "hot spot" in the fly's name. Do not trim away the excess marabou. Leave it there for a future step.

Step 3: Select a hackle feather that matches the marabou color, stroke out the fibers, and fold them in preparation for a typical wet-hackle application. Tie the feather tip to the hook at the forward end of the hot spot using anchor wraps behind and in front of the marabou.

Step 4: Grasp the marabou and thread together with the right thumb/forefinger while maintaining control of the bobbin in palm of the hand. Pull the thread/marabou forward parallel with the shank and press the red button to rotate the hook. This maneuver will form a strand of marabou chenille with a thread core.

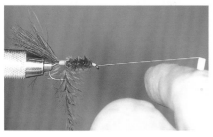

Step 5: Next bring the marabou chenille perpendicular with the shank and wrap it forward forming the body. Tie it off and trim away the waste end. Note: With a little practice the previous step and this one can be completed without stopping the vise's rotation. Wrap several turns of thread over the trimmed marabou then place a half hitch to keep everything from coming apart as we prepare to palmer the hackle. Illustrated here is the Bob Lay method of applying the hackle while employing a finger as a bobbin rest. Bob likes to use his little finger and I prefer the ring finger; with a little practice you'll find the one that works best for you.

Step 6: Press the red button and watch the hackle spring to life around the body while palmering it forward to the hook eye. Tie off the feather and trim away the waste end. Build a fairly substantial head, whip-finish, and trim the thread from the hook. Apply a coating of Aqua Head to complete the fly. The head and the tag both form "hot spots" and have proven very attractive to fish for Gretchen and me. A bead-head version has also been quite successful for us.

Backward Peacock Bugger - Universal Vise

I've really been looking forward to tying on this vise because it brings me into the realm of rotary tying I really know quite well. It's unfortunate the Universal Vise did not survive through time to remain on the market today because it had some really neat features. It's one of the few vises that could be "true" rotary as well as "full" rotation based simply on the position the tier adjusted the jaws. When using it as a true rotary tool the tension adjustment was directly adjacent to the rotating spool or spindle. I found I could adjust my rotating/tying speed by using my left forefinger to chase the spool slowly through a delicate maneuver then really speed things up using the spindle to scoot through a less demanding application.

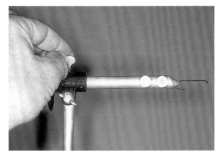

The jaw was lowered to make the vise true rotary. Notice the tension adjustment between my forefinger and thumb.

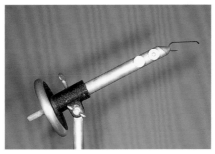

By tilting the jaws up at an angle the vise was converted to a full rotary rather than true rotary.

Use the forefinger on the wheel to slowly move through a delicate maneuver.

The Backward Peacock Bugger is a pattern right out of our fly boxes. It has accounted for more of my fish than any other wet pattern with the Hot Spot Bugger running a very close second. They both have produced many fish covering a wide range of species for Gretchen and me. Also on this pattern we start learning techniques appropriate for any of today's rotary vises. And that's what this book is really all about, techniques to make you more versatile and competent with your rotary vise.

Turning the spindle really speeds up the process.

Backward Peacock Bugger

Hook:	Size 2 to 16, streamer or wet style
Thread:	Black
Rib:	Thread
Tail:	Black or brown marabou
Hackle:	Black, brown, or color of choice
Body:	Peacock herl
Head:	Thread, optional bead head

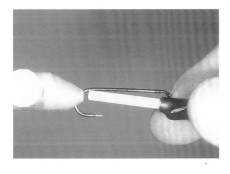

Step 1: Up to this point we've not talked much about putting on a thread base but here is as good a time as any to illustrate a great feature a true rotary vise brings to the tier. Let's start a thread base just behind the hook eye with three or four wraps. Trim off the waste end and spin the vise to apply the thread base. Notice how I effectively avoid the hook point while applying thread all the way to the end of the shank by positioning my bobbin to take advantage of the span of the gape. This technique works great on hooks larger than size twenty but has little application on those smaller fellows.

Step 2: Select a marabou feather and tie it on the hook to form a tail that is about as long as the shank. Trim off the excess marabou leaving the thread at the end of the shank. Notice I like a fairly sparse tail on my Buggers. Pluck several strands of peacock herl all about the same length and tie them to the end of the shank by their tips. Before continuing, select a hackle feather and strip the fuzzy material from the base of the stem. Set it aside for the moment. Bring the herls in line with the tying thread, hold them and the thread together along the shank, and spin the vise to form peacock chenille.

Step 3: Bring the peacock chenille perpendicular to the hook shank and rotate the vise to apply half the body stopping in the center of the hook. Do not let go of the chenille because it will unwind into this awful mess. Pick up the prepared hackle feather and bind it to the hook (tip pointing forward) with the chenille using a couple wraps to anchor it. Then continue rotating the vise while constructing the last half of the body. Notice you are also binding the feather to the hook as well. Tie off the body, trim the excess peacock herl,and clip off the waste end of the hackle feather. If you accidentally leave an ugly hackle stem end exposed in the middle of your beautiful peacock body you can cover it up with a felt tip marker but this seldom happens.

Step 4: If the tying thread is not behind the hackle feather then make sure it is because I'm going to wrap the hackle from the front to the back of the hook. Remember, the thread always leads the process when advancing it with any material. Take one turn of hackle in front of the thread close to the hook eye then hold it and the bobbin together in preparation to palmer the hackle. Notice the separation between the hackle and thread.

Step 5: Rotate the vise palmering the hackle to the end of the hook shank. Take a couple of thread wraps to anchor the feather then trim the waste tip.

Step 6: Hold the thread at about a seventy-degree angle. Rotate the vise while advancing the thread rib to the front of the fly.

Step 7: Build a head, apply a whip-finish, and trim the thread from the hook. Place a drop of Aqua Head on the whip-finish to complete the fly.

Well the last few pages were an introduction to rotary tying. I certainly had a lot of fun bringing these flies and techniques to you. In the first pattern we learned how to construct the body and hackle all at one time. That technique works equally well on modern vises as it did seventy years ago on a treadle vise. The second fly demonstrated the construction of marabou chenille then we followed with a third fly reinforcing that technique with a different material. Don't forget the front-to-back tying with the palmered hackle on the Backward Peacock Bugger; this is not the last time you'll see that technique. Now let's move on to flies and techniques using modern-day tools and vises.

Several Things to Discuss

In the previous chapter there are several items I didn't review because we were just having some fun with three pieces of history. Now it's time to get into the heart of rotary tying using modern-day tools.

The vises Gretchen and I included herein were loaned to us by the various manufacturers or were already in our inventory. In some cases, like Ron Abby's vises (Dyna-King), Norm Norlander's (Nor-Vise), or Bernie Griffin's, they requested we demonstrate on their newer models rather than an older one. That was certainly fine with us and also provided many hours of entertainment "playing" with the new tools. Some manufacturers equipment is not featured because they elected to not participate for one reason or another. Last we may have just missed giving a company the opportunity to be a part of the book and if that happened I sincerely apologize for the oversight. It certainly was not intended. With that said let's get to the items I wanted to discuss.

True-Rotary Versus Full-Rotation

Let's start by defining and illustrating the difference between true-rotary and full-rotation vises. A true-rotary vise will rotate the hook with its shank on axis. What this means is the shank will not move up or down while rotating the vise, it will be the exact distance from the tying bench surface no matter where it is in the rotation. Pictured here are two of Bernie Griffin's vises, an Odyssey (true-rotary) and a Patriot Cam (full-rotation). I've tilted the jaws in the Patriot down so they are

parallel to the tying bench surface. Next I rotate the jaws on each vise one-half turn. The hook shank in the Odyssey's jaws remains in the same position while those in the Patriot do not. Now I'll return the Patriot's jaws to their regular forty-five- degree angle and repeat the experiment. Again the one hook does not change axis while the other points its nose to the sky.

The Right Direction

One of the first things I learned when I started tying rotary was the direction I had to turn the vise to apply materials. It was the exact opposite of what I thought it would be. Let's complete one turn of thread using regular hand tying techniques and then apply the next by rotating the vise. With the thread already mounted on the hook, I'll start by securing the bobbin with my right hand and bring it toward my body. The rotation continues as it reaches the top of the hook shank and then drops over the other side going away from me. The turn is complete when I reach the starting point at the bottom of the hook. That single rotation is the way most fly tiers apply thread to a hook. Yes, Gretchen and I have met several fly tiers who wrap their thread the opposite direction as described here but they are the exceptions rather than the rule.

The next thing we need to explore then is adding that same turn of thread by rotating the vise while holding the right hand/bobbin stationery. The first time I tried this function I started by pulling forward on the rotating mechanism with my left hand and going up and

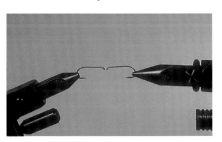

The Griffin's Odyssey (true-rotary) is on the left and the Patriot (full-rotation) is on the right. With the Patriot jaws positioned parallel with the tying table, the hook shanks in both vises are in line.

When I rotate both vises one-half turn, the hook shank in the Odyssey vise remains on axis.

If I reposition the Patriot's jaws at the more traditional forty-five-degree angle and rotate the jaws of each vise again, it become very evident which vise is a true-rotary and the one that is full-rotation.

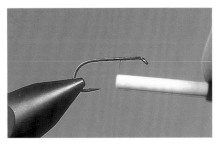

I'm starting a single rotation around the hook by bringing my hand toward me.

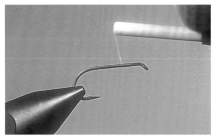

The rotation is completed as I go over the top of the shank and drop down the other side away from me.

To wrap a single turn of thread on the hook by rotating the vise I start by pushing the handle away from me. This is exactly the opposite of what I thought it would be when I started to learn rotary-tying techniques.

As I reach the top of the turn I must pull toward me to complete it.

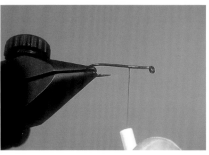

Following this same turn of thread by focusing on the hook, as I push the rotating handle away from me the hook point also moves in that direction.

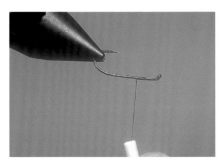

Here the hook point has reached the top of the rotation and starts down the other side as I pull toward me on the rotating handle.

over just like I did with my right hand. That is exactly the wrong direction to turn the vise for applying materials/thread but it's a great way to remove items if that is the objective. To rotate the vise in the proper direction I push the handle away from my body until I reach the top of the turn then pull toward me to complete it. That sure seemed backward when I first started rotary tying but over the years it has become a habit and today seems quite natural. Now when I apply a thread turn to the hook using the vise my right hand remains still while the left rotates the handle one complete turn going in the direction I reviewed a couple of sentences ago. The thread wrap is done when the vise has made one complete rotation.

Crisscross Application

I was going to call the way we must rotate the vise to get the materials on the hook backward turns until I stumbled on the next bit of information. What I'm going to discuss here are crisscross thread wraps. For almost forty years I never gave them much thought until I started teaching rotary-tying classes about ten years ago. In verbalizing an answer to a question from a student about the direction a material goes on a hook, I had

to really take a new look at the crisscross wrap. The material/thread seems to go on the hook in the opposite direction when it is wrapped to the back of the shank rather than when advanced forward. For a bit that discovery really stopped me in my tracks. It was not possible! My hand was moving in the same clock-wise direction around the hook no matter which way it was traveling. However, the forward turns crossed over the backward wraps. If they were going the same direction they would have paralleled each other and this definitely did not happen. The only way I could make the forward turns parallel the backward was to reverse wrap the thread. I content the thread/material changes from clockwise to counter-clockwise based on the direction of application however some of my fly-tying friends (my lovely wife Gretchen included) disagree with that premise. It really doesn't make any difference whether you agree/disagree with my assumption, the fact that forward turns cross over backward (crisscross) is really useful information to me when I am applying materials to a hook. Let me give you an example. A peacock herl body reinforced with a counter wrapped wire rib can be constructed using a couple of different methods. The first way is tie both materials at the back of the hook, wrap the peacock forward in a clockwise direction, and then wind the wire rib forward using counter clockwise wraps (a method familiar to many tiers). The second way is to tie the peacock on at the front of the hook and the wire for the rib at the back. When the herl is wrapped back and the wire is wrapped forward over the peacock the same thing happens, the rib anchors the body to the hook shank (refer to Chapter 3, steps 4,5 and 6). As we advance through these pages you will come to understand what an important technique the crisscross wrap is to rotary as well as standard fly tying.

The Bobbin Rest

If I were a betting man I'd wager most fly tiers who tie on a rotating vise seldom use the bobbin rest. I admit I used to be one who was guilty of ignoring this useful part of my vise. Norm Norlander (Nor-Vise developer) finally convinced me of its value especially if combined with his awesome Automatic Bobbin. The two units, when used as a team, really do add a dimension to rotary tying and save the tier a lot time. Rewinding excess thread pulled off the spool to reach an adjacent bobbin rest can be a real pain in the ... (you pick the

body part)! I'll talk about the Automatic Bobbin in further detail a bit later and you'll find me using it through the book.

During the years I did not regularly use the bobbin rest I often positioned my hands to act as one during some tying functions. Several years ago my good friend Bob Lay illustrated his technique using his little finger to support the bobbin during some tying maneuvers. It doesn't work in every situation but certainly has its place. Personally I like to turn my hand over and use the middle finger as a bobbin rest. It just works better for me. Whichever method you decide to use I suggest you spend some time perfecting one or the other. Better yet, develop a technique of your own and send the information to me. I'm always interested in new ideas.

Another type of finger placement you can use is one I call the "traveling bobbin rest." In an earlier chapter I mentioned that the thread always leads the process when it is applied at the same time as a material. The traveling bobbin rest accomplishes the same thing but allows the tier to tie off the material much easier. To perform this function hold the material with the right thumb and forefinger then use the next finger to support the thread/

You can see the turns I'm placing as I wrap forward on the shank cross over the turns I placed winding toward the back of the hook. We call these crisscross wraps. They literally bind each other to the hook.

The only way I can get my forward turns to parallel the backward is by using a bodkin to reverse my direction. Then by wrapping my hand backward I can parallel the thread turns placed when I wrapped toward the rear of the hook.

The Norlander Automatic Bobbin used with a bobbin rest adds a special dimension to rotary tying.

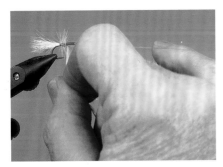

The Bob Lay method of using the little finger as a bobbin rest.

I much prefer turning my hand over and using the middle finger as a bobbin rest.

The thread always leads when it is applied at the same time as a material. Here I am wrapping the hackle from back to front and the thread leads the way.

bobbin. In the illustration I've had to twist my hand so you can see what I'm doing but this technique really does keep the thread in front of the material.

The traveling bobbin rest sets us up for the last "free hand technique," the "drop tie off." To accomplish it all you do is drop the bobbin from the traveling bobbin rest (finger) at the location on the shank where you want to tie off the material. Then wrap the material (remember you are rotating the vise to accomplish this) two more turns past the drop zone. Then when you let go of the material it unwinds those two turns and is securely anchored with two thread wraps.

Now let's move on to the fun part, tying flies on the various vises. I had planned on presenting each manufacturer in alphabetical order but I had one dilemma. I think Norlander's Automatic Bobbin is a very important part of rotary tying so I moved him to the head of the pack so I could review some of the positives it brings to the tying bench.

Here the middle finger is used as a traveling bobbin rest.

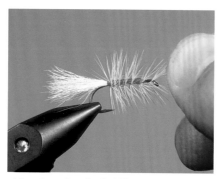

After dropping the bobbin, wrap two more turns to complete the tie off.

When I let go of the feather the turns forward of the tie-off position come unwrapped, but the hackle is anchored by two thread turns.

Tie Better Flies Faster is the theme Norm Norlander presents on behalf of his fly-tying system focused around the Nor-Vise and the Automatic Bobbin. Norm's fly-tying system is one of the most unique I've had the pleasure to see and operate. Flies really are constructed much faster using this system; they literally spin off the vise, no pun intended.

For years Norm's day job was as an engineer for the R & D Lab at Weyerhaeuser. There in 1965, working on his lunch hours, he developed the prototype of what you see here today. He wasn't a skilled machinist so the

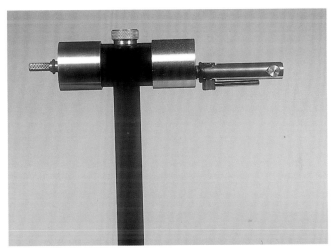

Tie Better Flies Faster with a Nor-Vise.

original was somewhat crude but worked and the design concept remains today. Before long his fishing buddies also wanted one of his vises and a part-time hobby was born. In 1972 a friend who sold drift boats invited Norm to set up a card table in his booth and demonstrate his vise. He sold his first one that year to Ken Jarvis. Norm and Ken became great friends fishing together all over the world. (Ken passed away early in 2003 and is missed by many of us in the fly-fishing business.) I met Norm and Ken at a Federation of Fly Fishers Conclave in West Yellowstone, Montana in the mid 80s where they were demonstrating and selling the vise. I fell in love with it the first time I saw it, but several years would pass before I could afford one.

About ten years ago Norm retired from his day job and devoted himself to producing a system of tying tools that complement the Nor-Vise and Automatic Bobbin. I know many of you reviewing these pages have seen him "spinning his magic" at trade shows all across the country. He is one of a few real masters of true-rotary tying.

In 1990, after countless prototypes, Norm was issued patents for the Automatic Bobbin. This bobbin really makes the Nor-Vise System work. I feel it is the heart of modern-day rotary tying. You will see me using it throughout these pages. The Automatic Bobbin is the reason I started the tying section of the book by demonstrating with Norm's equipment. An Automatic Bobbin is not required to tie flies by rotating the hook but it is darned sure helpful.

The bobbin works in conjunction with the bobbin rest and Norlander's is quite unique. Norm calls it the "thread post" and besides acting as a bobbin rest it is also the location where he stores the bobbin in what I call the "ready mode," under tension and ready to go.

Let's take a moment to set up a new bobbin. It comes as part of a kit that includes a bobbin with a spool, three extra spools, and thread loading hub. Loading the spare spool is quite easy using an electric drill. Just slip it on the supplied hub, place it in the

Norm's thread post acts as a bobbin rest.

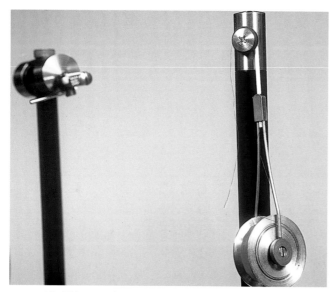

A bobbin stored on the thread post in the ready mode.

chuck of an electric drill, and transfer the thread from a regular spool. Slip the spool on the bobbin hub, hold the two small arbors between the thumb and forefinger, pull on the thread, and let got of it. If the thread retracts, the spool is mounted correctly on the hub. If the thread does not retract then slip the spool off the hub and turn it over. Mount the hub in the bobbin frame and take a loop

The Automatic Bobbin Kit includes a bobbin/ spool, three extra spools, and a thread-loading hub.

around one of the legs. You are now ready to use this great tool to tie flies. Note: If you are refilling a spool already mounted on the bobbin just remove the hub/ spool and place one of the short arbors in the drill chuck. Also Norm recommends filling the spool about two-thirds full.

Before I actually tie a fly let's talk about some of the features of the Nor-Vise. Starting at the back is the rotating arbor and next to it is the rear hub with a

retaining ring mounted between the two. When the rear hub is pulled tight back against the retaining ring the vise is in the free spinning mode and when it is pushed forward about one-fourth inch it is locked in one of four positions: up, down, or to the sides. Located between the two hubs is the tension adjustment allowing the fly tier rotating speeds from very fast to a slow crawl. At the very front are the cam-operated jaws.

The thread hub loaded in a spare spool.

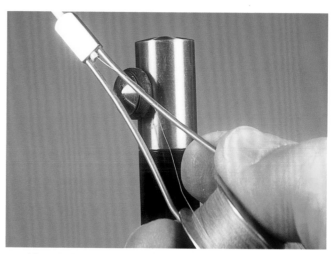

After placing the loaded spool in the vise frame take a loop around one of the legs before threading in through the ceramic barrel.

The rotating arbor is at the back of the vise.

When the rear hub is pulled tight against the retaining ring on the rotating arbor the vise is in the free-spin mode.

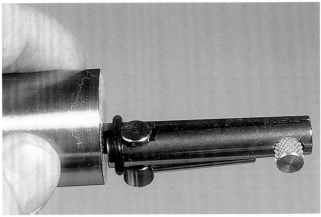

At the very front are the cam-operated jaws.

Chapter 5: The Norlander Company

Orange Asher

I selected this fly to illustrate again the traveling bobbin rest as part of the free hand style of rotary tying. Because I'm not using the thread post, the bobbin I'm employing is a standard ceramic rather than the Automatic Bobbin. I find a standard bobbin works ok if I'm not using the cradle/rest but as soon as one is brought into the equation my frustration level rises. Manually rewinding the thread can get to be a real pain, you know!

On this pattern I'm winding the hackle from the back to the front of the fly. According to Norm Norlander this practice (wrapping the hackle in one direction) can cause your leader to twist if the fly is drug through the water. He claims the "one direction" hackle causes the fly to spin if submerged in the water column. I've not personally experienced this problem with the Orange Asher but I usually fish it dry. When it starts to move cross the current I recast the fly to once again present a drag-free drift so it doesn't spend much time moving through the water.

Every fly Gretchen and I selected for presentation within these pages was chosen because it not only taught a lesson but it also a fly in which we have a lot of confidence. We do tie our version of the Asher with a tag not included in the original pattern. What can I say? Like many fly tiers we are always experimenting; nothing is sacred. Also, Gretchen and I use a lot of size A unwaxed Danville thread. We think it is the best single strand floss ever made.

Orange Asher

Hook:	Size 8 to 20, standard dry fly
Thread:	Orange size A, un-waxed
Tag:	Thread
Body:	Thread
Hackle:	Grizzly, palmered one direction
Head:	Thread

Step 1: Place the hook in the vise and start a thread base just behind the eye. Wrap a couple turns and trim off the waste end. Grasp the bobbin in the right hand and spin the vise to apply the thread. Remember we are using size A thread like it was floss. See how smooth the body is when the vise does the rotating rather than the hand. Every time your hand goes around the hook a twist is placed in the thread in the section between the spool and the shank. When you rotate the hook by turning the vise the thread remains flat. Also notice how I avoid the danger of the hook point by my positioning of the bobbin.

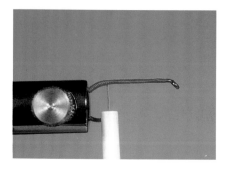

Step 2: Wrap the thread down into the hook bend and back to the end of the shank. This section of wrapped thread forms the tag. We include it on a lot of our flies and they all seem to catch fish. I hand-wrapped the tag rather than rotating the vise. Notice the thread turns are not as smooth in the tag as they are in the thread base placed in the last step.

Step 3: Select a grizzly hackle feather and strip the fibers from the base of the stem. Tie it to the hook with two snug wraps. Now I'll bring the middle finger into position and drape the thread over it. It becomes the traveling bobbin rest.

Step 4: Next I'm taking a wrap of hackle around the hook and grasping the feather with my thumb and forefinger. I still have the thread over the traveling bobbin rest (middle finger) but it is hidden from the camera's view by the other two fingers.

Step 5: After rotating the vise several turns I reach the center of the hook. Notice that I've tied the remaining portion of the stem to the hook and wrapped a body in the process.

Step 6: Here I've completed the palmered hackle, dropped the bobbin, and rotated the vise two more turns thus tying off the feather.

Step 7: A whip-finish completes the fly. I like to place a drop of Aqua Head on the whip-finish but that's a personal choice.

Chapter 5: The Norlander Company

Red Asher

Gretchen and I learned about the Orange Asher when we lived in Colorado. It was quite popular with many of the locals especially on the Gunnison River. Like all fly tiers it didn't take us long to change material colors and some of those experiments proved successful as well. Various Asher-style flies found their way into our personal fly boxes in colors like red, chartreuse, burnt orange, and black. We used various colored hackle and I found I liked black as a sometimes substitute for the standard grizzly. The Red Asher was born or so we thought.

One day we met a fellow fishing the Gunnison River above the Black Canyon who seemed to really have the fish "dialed in." I wandered over to talk with him hoping to find out what pattern was on the end of his tippet. I asked if he would mind sharing with us what fly he was using and he responded it was a size fourteen Bloody Butcher. Darned if his fly didn't look just like the one I called Red Asher. I asked where he had gotten it and he told me at a shop in the Denver area. I thanked him and went back to fishing with a Red Asher/Bloody Butcher tied to my tippet and yes, my catch rate really improved for the rest of the day. I was puzzled a bit because I thought a Bloody Butcher was a wet fly developed over one hundred fifty years ago by two fellows named Moon and Jewhurst. Jewhurst was a butcher by trade and his occupation eventually took over the fly's name as well.

No matter what the correct name I present the fly here because I can effectively illustrate the application of a back-and-forth hackle. If Norm Norlander is correct and a palmered hackle wrapped in one direction can cause a fly to twist the leader then here is an alternative style that shouldn't cause that problem.

Red Asher

Hook:	Size 8 to 20, standard dry fly
Thread:	Red size A, un-waxed
Tag:	Thread
Hackle:	Black, palmered two directions
Head:	Thread

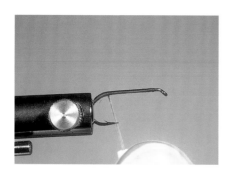

Step 1: Start a thread base just behind the hook eye with a couple of thread turns and trim the waste end. Note that I'm using the Norlander Automatic Bobbin. Hold the bobbin in the right hand and turn the vise with the left. When you reach the end of the shank continue the thread base down into the hook bend and then back to the end of the shank preparing the tag in the process.

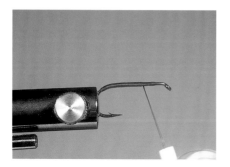

Step 2: Advance the thread back along the hook until reaching the one-third point on the shank. Remember I'm holding the bobbin hand stationary and rotating the vise.

Step 3: Prepare a black hackle feather by stripping the fuzzy fibers from the end of the stem. I suggest exposing about a half inch. Slip the stripped part of the stem under the thread then up on top of the shank.

Step 4: Slide the stem to the bottom of the shank then pull on the feather so the stripped part slips forward until it almost pulls out from under the single thread turn.

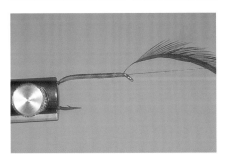

Step 5: Rotate the vise applying the thread over the exposed hackle stem while constructing the last part of the body. Place the thread/bobbin over the thread post. Notice that I place a single half hitch just in front of the feather stem before placing the bobbin on the post.

Step 6: I'm holding the feather with my right hand and rotating the vise with my left. Also I'm applying the hackle in fairly open turns so I have room to fill in those gapes on the return trip. I also have to pay particular attention to the hook point to avoid cutting the feather when I approach the end of the shank.

Step 7: When I reach the end of the shank I start the return trip filling the spaces I left in the previous step. Notice how the crisscross feather wraps produce a really attractive palmered hackle and because they cross over each other the fly is more durable.

Step 8: Complete the forward hackle application, tie it off, and trim away the waste end. Apply a whip-finish then coat it with Aqua Head to complete the fly. It is very easy to evenly apply the head cement by spinning the vise while holding the bodkin stationary.

EZY Prince Nymph (Bead Head)

$\mathbf{D}$uring my years as a Montana guide Gretchen and I developed a series of patterns that we called EZY Trout Flies. The EZY Prince Nymph was one of my daily "go to" patterns to ensure my customers had a good day of fishing. It is also very easy to tie using rotary-tying techniques.

Here we will learn one method for making peacock chenille to strengthen the fragile material then we'll improve durability even more by applying a counter rib. Both operations are much easier using rotary-tying techniques rather than stationary.

I also want you to notice I'm using orange thread. That was a color especially effective on the Yellowstone River. (On the Madison River the fish seemed to like lime green better than orange.)

EZY Prince Nymph (Bead Head)

Hook:	Size 6 to 16, 2XL nymph hook
Thread:	Orange
Tail:	Brown Antron yarn, combed
Rib:	Oval silver tinsel, optional
Body:	Peacock herl
Wing:	White Antron yarn, combed
Hackle:	Brown
Head:	Gold bead

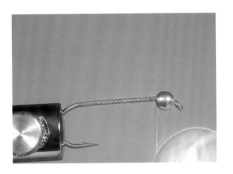

Step 1: Slip a gold bead on the hook then place it in the vise. Lay down the thread base the covers the complete hook shank stopping directly behind the bead.

Step 2: Select a length of white Antron yarn and tie it to the hook directly behind the bead. Bind it to the shank up to the center of the hook and trim off the waste end. Now select a length of brown Antron yarn and tie it to the shank in the center of the hook. Bind it to the hook up to the end of the shank. Trim both segments of Antron yarn so each is about as long as the portion of the shank behind the bead. Use a mustache comb to fuzz out the brown yarn extending beyond the hook completing the tail portion of the fly.

Step 3: Advance the tying thread forward by rotating the vise to a position just behind the bead. Trim a several inch section of silver, oval tinsel and bind it to the hook on the underside of the shank. Quite frankly I find tying the tinsel to the bottom of the hook is easier for me using stationary techniques rather than rotating the vise. If any of you find a good way to accomplish using rotary-tying techniques I sure would appreciate learning your method. Once the tinsel is bound to the hook all the way to the end of the shank store the loose end in the slot between the jaws. Norm recommends using this slot as a material keeper.

Step 4: Select several peacock herls and tie them to the hook at the end of the shank by their tips. Make sure the tying thread is positioned tight against the herls after the tie-in operation. Grasp the thread and the herls with the right thumb and fore finger while holding the bobbin in the palm of the same hand. Bring the thread/herl straight forward and spin the vise to form a section of peacock chenille with a thread core.

Step 5: Bring the peacock chenille back so it is forms a ninety-degree angle with the hook shank. Rotate the vise to form a body then tie if off just behind the bead. With a little practice you will be able to complete Steps Four & Five without ever stopping the vise.

Step 6: Trim off the waste ends of the peacock herl then place a half hitch between the incomplete wing and the bead. Store the bobbin on the thread post and retrieve the tinsel stored in the jaws slot. Bring the tinsel around so it is perpendicular with the hook shank then move it forward slightly and spin the vise to apply the rib. If you spin the vise in the opposite direction that you did when applying the body material you will end up with a counter rib, which is what I did here. If you don't want a counter rib, then spin the vise in the same direction as that used in applying the body. Retrieve the bobbin from the thread post and tie off the tinsel.

Step 7: Trim off the waste end of the tinsel. Pull the wing material back and tie it down forming a Trude style Antron wing.

Step 8: Select a brown hackle and strip the fuzzy material from the base of the stem. Tie it on the hook behind the bead and wrap a two-turn hackle collar. Tie it off and trim away the waste end. Execute a whip-finish, trim off the thread, and apply a coat of Aqua Head. Comb out the wing to complete the fly.

Chapter 5: The Norlander Company

— 6 —

Dyna-King, Inc.

I just returned to the keyboard after checking our fly-tying room. In it we have at least one vise from just about every company in the USA involved in the fly-tying industry. We have six vises manufactured by Ron Abby's company Dyna-King, Inc. Understand we use vises from different manufacturers to complete different functions based on whatever commercial order we are working on at the time. We use Danvises, Griffin's vises, and those from "awesome Abby" as well. The fact we have six of Ron's vises identifies that both Gretchen and I use them because the count includes two each of three different styles.

In the early 80s commercial fly tier Grant F. King encouraged Ron to produce a fly tying vise and in 1981 the Professional became Dyna-King's first production model. Starting in a 500-square-foot shop, Ron, wife Lenora, and son Mark brought Abby Precision Manufacturing into being. The new vise was well received by the fly-tying public (including me) and in a short time Abby needed to expand his manufacturing facility.

The company continued to grow until in 1998 the family owned business incorporated under the name, Dyna-King, Inc. Today Dyna-King distributes world-wide twenty-two different vise models and over twenty-five tying accessories. The popular Barracuda (introduced in 1997) and the new Barracuda Junior Trekker are the two Abby vises I feature in the next several pages.

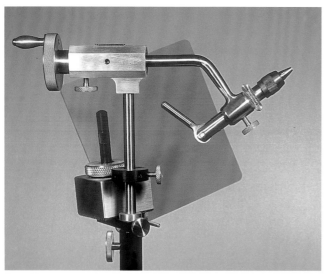

The Barracuda was introduced in 1997.

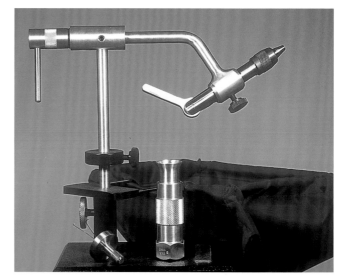

The Barracuda Trakker Junior is a new addition to the Abby line of vises.

Peacock Woolly Bugger (Bead Head)

If you were to peruse my personal fly assortment in my chest pack or the boxes I use in the drift boat with customers you would immediately notice I have a bunch of bead-head, peacock buggers. It's a pattern that catches a lot of fish for Gretchen and me; we consider it a "go to fly" when ever we delve into new waters where we have little or no idea what will produce. Often it produces so well we don't have to search further for a fly that is attractive to the fish. This is probably no surprise to many of you because some type of Bugger more than likely resides in your fly boxes or at the end of your tippet.

You'll note in the materials list below we tie it in a range of sizes from size two to sixteen. That's because it is equally effective in small sizes as a nymph or in larger sizes tied to represent a baitfish. Yes, I admit it is a very easy pattern that most of you already know how to tie. My purpose here though is to share with you a couple techniques the pattern really illustrates quite well; another (non rotary) method for making peacock chenille and a way to strengthen palmered hackle.

Peacock Woolly Bugger

Hook:	Hook size 2 to 16, 3XL streamer/nymph hook
Thread:	Black
Tail:	Black or brown marabou
Rib:	Copper wire
Body:	Peacock herl
Hackle:	Black or grizzly, palmered
Head:	Gold bead

Step 1: Slip a gold bead on the hook and place it in the vise jaws. Apply a thread base that starts at the bead and stops at the end of the shank. Tie a section of copper wire to the underside of the hook while wrapping the thread forward to meet the bead. Select a marabou feather and bind it to the top of the hook to form a tail that is as long as shank. Trim any waste ends. Most of the functions in the step are easier to accomplish using stationary tying practices with the exception of the thread base. It goes on really smooth using the rotating feature of the Barracuda Junior Trekker. The thread is left just behind the bead in preparation for the next step.

Step 2: Prepare a black saddle feather by stripping the fuzzy fibers from the base of the stem. Tie it to the front of the hook just behind the bead. Wrap the thread to the end of the shank and tie several peacock herls on by their tips. Form the thread into a dubbing loop and grasp it with a test clip or one of BT's EZY Hackle Pliers. Bring the peacock herl strands together and grasp them also with the clip. Make sure they are longer than the thread so the herl forms a "D" shape with the dubbing loop the short side. Wrap the tying thread forward to meet the hackle then place both in the bobbin rest, thread on top of the feather.

Step 3: Rotate the clip several turns causing the herls to wind around the thread core forming peacock chenille. Rotate the vise several turns to construct a body from the newly, formed chenille. Notice that the hackle and thread are also twisting around each other. Don't be concerned, this is supposed to happen and will in fact make the fly much more durable when it is complete.

Step 4: Grasp the twisted thread/hackle with the right hand and push the bobbin rest out of the way. Take one turn of hackle/thread around the hook to tie off the body then remove the clip. For now don't worry about trimming the waste ends of peacock remaining from the body. We'll deal with them later when it's time to whip-finish the fly. Rotate the vise several turns winding the hackle from the front of the hook to the back while placing evenly spaced wraps. Untangle the feather/thread at the back of the hook, tie off the hackle, and trim the excess.

Step 5: Bring the copper rib even with the thread and wrap the two forward forming the rib; remember to rotate the vise to complete the operation. Tie off the copper wire and trim it from the hook along with the peacock herl left from the previous step.

Step 6: Pull the bobbin out from the hook about eight inches and trim the thread so it is six inches long. Lay the bobbin aside for the next fly. Using the right forefinger and middle finger form a loop as if you were going to place a half hitch with your hand. Move the half hitch loop into position and rotate the vise to complete a whip-finish. Pull the knot tight and trim off the waste end. Think about how tough this fly is, the number of times we've crisscrossed materials and thread back over each other. It's darned near bomb proof!

Stimulator

I'd be willing to bet that more than half of the fly-fishers who pursue trout have at least a few of this pattern in their fly box. It is considered an attractor fly and that is exactly its effect on fish, they are drawn to it like a magnet. I use it as a stonefly or caddisfly imitation simply matching the size and color of the insects available. When no hatch is evident I use it as a searching pattern, often rigged with a nymph on a dropper. More often than not my nymph of choice is a Peacock Woolly Bugger or an EZY Prince Nymph. I like it tied in orange, olive, peacock, lime, and hare's ear for colors with a size range from four to twenty-two.

Not only is it attractive to the fish but it is pleasing to my eye as well. I fell in love with the appearance of the curved hook when it first came on the market and today, many years later it still looks good to me. I think the Stimulator hook (that's what I've come to call it)

and a Bartleet Salmon Fly Iron are two of the most elegant hooks available to the fly tier. There is certainly nothing wrong with me. Here I am allowing the alluring curve of a hook to steer me away from my real purpose, tying flies.

In the rotary tying world the Stimulator provides a really good platform on which to practice several techniques. On this pattern I'm going to demonstrate a technique often used when applying more than one material to a part of the fly, tying in two directions. I'm also going to introduce you to the idea of moving the tying hand around the hook, as you would during stationary fly dressing and at the same time turning the vise. This two-part technique really speeds up the process and also allows the tier to inspect all sides of the fly during the construction process. Last but not least we'll continue practicing the drop tie off and the rotating vise whip-finish.

Stimulator

Hook:	Size 4 to 22, curved shank
Thread:	Orange
Tail:	Elk hair
Body:	Orange dubbing
Body hackle:	Brown
Wing:	Elk hair
Head:	Peacock herl
Front hackle:	Grizzly

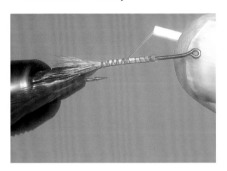

Step 1: Place the hook in the vise and apply a thread base that covers the back two-thirds of the hook shank. Cut a small bundle of elk hair from the hide and remove the under fur and short fibers. Even the tips in a hair stacker then tie the hair to the top of the shank forming a tail about as long as the distance of the gape. Stop the thread even with the hook point then trim off the waste hair ends. Select a brown saddle hackle that is sized for a hook smaller than the one in the vise. Strip the fuzzy fibers from the end of the stem and tie it to the underside of the shank directly above the hook point using two thread turns. Now we will practice advancing the thread forward by hand as well as rotating the vise to speed up the process. Stop at the one-third point and leave the bobbin there for the next step. Now, rotating the vise and wrapping with the tying hand wasn't too hard was it?

Step 2: Apply wax to the thread, touch the dubbing to the coated area, and twist it to form a strand of yarn with a thread core. Starting at the one-third point, wrap the dubbed thread back to meet the hackle thus forming the body. Rotate the vise while hand wrapping to again practice this two-way technique. I like to stop rotating the vise with the hook up side down a bit short of the end of the body then finish wrapping the last couple of turns by hand. This is one way to avoid cutting the thread on the hook point.

Step 3: Wind the last couple of turns to complete the body. Rest the thread on the traveling bobbin rest (the middle finger tip) and grasp the feather with the thumb and forefinger. Rotate the vise to palmer the hackle forward to the front of the body. After reaching the front of the body drop the thread from the traveling bobbin rest and rotate the vise two more turns to tie off the feather.

Step 4: Trim off the excess hackle then wrap the thread forward about three turns. Select, clean, and stack a clump of elk hair. Tie it to the hook to form a wing that is long enough to reach the end of the tail. Trim off the excess hair at a fairly severe angle. Prepare a grizzly saddle feather by stripping the fuzzy material from the base of the stem. It should be a size smaller to match the fibers on the brown feather. Tie it to the hook at the front of the wing.

Chapter 6: Dyna-King, Inc.

Step 5: Wrap the thread forward to the hook eye covering the trimmed wing ends in the process. Select several strands of peacock herl and tie them to the front of the hook shank by their tips. Grasp the herl and the thread with the right thumb and forefinger. Pull the unit out straight in front of the hook and rotate the vise to construct a strand of peacock chenille with a thread core. Bring the chenille back perpendicular to the hook shank and rotate the vise to wrap it back to meet the grizzly hackle.

Step 6: Finish wrapping the peacock herl, tie it off in front of the hackle, and trim the waste ends. Bring the hackle and thread together (thread to the front) and rotate the vise to palmer the hackle forward over the head of the fly. Tie off the hackle and trim the excess feather. Wrap a thread head and place one half hitch. Clip the thread from the bobbin leaving a six-inch section at the front of the hook. On the last fly I demonstrated the rotary hand whip with my fingers positioned on the underside of the hook. The method I prefer is with them positioned above the hook like I'm illustrating here. Complete the whip-finish and trim the thread from the hook. Finish the fly with a coating of Aqua Head.

Regulator

Sometimes boredom can be the catalyst to inspiration and that's how this pattern was born. Gretchen and I were working a fly-fishing show in Oregon; one that opens at ten in the morning and goes until ten at night. Sometimes the pace in the evening is fast with many people visiting our booth and other times the longest eight hours of the day is between nine and ten p.m. On one such evening I was just killing time tying a few flies for my own boxes or for friends. At that time a now departed friend Bob Curtis loved to fish with a Wright's Royal and I though I'd tie him a few during the slack time of the evening. Unfortunately I didn't have elk hair for the wing and decided to substitute calf tail for it. Of course, I tied it on a curved shank Stimulator style hook.

The fly looked kind of neat so I dressed a half dozen or so. Just as the show was closing this really neat guy stopped to chat and I ended up giving him a couple flies and my card with instructions to let me know how they worked. He assured me he was going fishing the next day and would give them a good test drive. About eight thirty the next evening he walked up to my booth and told me he had a great day until he lost both of them. He was back for more. In the process of selling him a half dozen he asked what the fly's name was. I told him it didn't have a name and he insisted I name it. Well to make a long story short the cubicle directly across from our booth was selling propane outdoor cooking devises and it had this great big sign that stated, "Newly Designed Regulator." You can figure out the rest but the fly did get a name.

It has since proved to be a great searching pattern on the freestone streams in central Idaho. In the course of testing the Regulator myself I changed the angle of the wing so it was tilted up ever so slightly. When I fish the fly I put BT's Float-EZY on the wing and hackle and our Sink-EZY on the back part of the body. That combination causes it to drift both in and on the water at the same time. I tie it in three colors: red, fire orange, and lime. The lime and orange are my favorites.

Regulator

Hook:	Size 6 to 20, curved shank
Thread:	Fire orange
Butt:	Peacock herl
Body:	Thread
Wing:	Calf body or tail hair
Head:	Peacock herl
Hackle:	Brown or grizzly

Step 1: Place the hook in the vise and wrap a thread base that starts at the one-third position and ends at a place on the shank directly above the point. Notice I'm taking great pains to lay down a very smooth thread base because it becomes the body in the next step. The rotating feature of the vise really helps with that little project. Select several peacock herls and tie them to the shank by their tips. Trim off the excess peacock and store the Automatic Bobbin in the Barracuda's bobbin rest. Notice I've changed from the Trekker Junior to the regular Barracuda. Rotate the vise to form peacock herl butt wrapping first down into the hook bend and then back to the starting point. I usually place a drop of Aqua Flex on the hook before wrapping the peacock to improve the durability of this fragile material.

Step 2: Retrieve the Automatic Bobbin from the rest and tie off the peacock herl. Trim the waste ends then advance the thread back to the one-third point. Again I flattened the thread and rotated the vise to construct a smooth body.

Step 3: Select, clean, and stack a clump of calf body or tail hair. Wrap the thread forward about three or four turns then tie the stacked hair to the shank to form a Trude style wing that ends even with the hook bend. Trim the hair at a severe angle to later provide a tapered hackle platform.

Step 4: Wrap the thread forward over the trimmed wing fibers ending at the hook eye. Place a half hitch then pull the thread back under the wing then forward again to the hook eye. When I apply tension to the thread under the wing I can adjust its angle. It is important to advance this "pull point" as far forward of the wings as possible. In so doing I can easily adjust the height/angle of the wing. If the "pull point" is too close to the wing it to will adjust the angle but also tends to kick the wing off center making the fly lop-sided.

Chapter 6: Dyna-King, Inc.

Step 5: Apply tension on the thread to tilt the wing up every so slightly then anchor it with a couple of turns at the hook eye. Wrap back to meet the wing, prepare a hackle by stripping the fuzzy fibers from the stem, and tie it to the underside of the hook. Wrap the thread forward and tie several peacock herls on the hook behind the eye. Grasp the herl and the thread with the right thumb and forefinger. Pull them out straight in front of the hook and rotate the vise to construct a strand of peacock chenille. Bring it back perpendicular to the hook shank and rotate the vise to wrap it back to meet the hackle.

Step 6: Finish wrapping the peacock head; tie it off, and trim the waste ends. Grasp the hackle and thread then rotate the vise to palmer the feather to the hook eye. Tie off the hackle and trim the excess feather. Apply a whip-finish using whatever method you choose but I sure recommend that you practice the hand applications reviewed earlier in this chapter. Notice the angle of the wing that causes the body to sink below the water's surface. If I had not thrown the loop under the wing you would not be able to see the body at the angle I shot the photograph.

Peacock Elk Hair Caddis

Remembering back over the years there is one fishing evening that always comes to mind. Ray Miles from Coeur d' Alene, Idaho and I were fishing the headwaters of the Clark Fork River in western Montana. Fishing through the day had been a bit slow but as evening approached a caddis hatch of fairly dark insects erupted in the small stream. Water that seemed fishless that afternoon exploded with feeding brown trout. We tied on peacock Elk Hair Caddis flies and proceeded to hook more darned fish than we had ever caught in a single outing before or since. The stream was small enough that we had to take turns casting to a feeding fish, hooking it, and leading the frisky brown trout downstream to be released. While I would be downstream fighting and releasing a fish, Ray would step into the water, hook a trout, and also lead it downstream. We repeated this process for the next hours catching and releasing many, many nice brown trout ranging in size from fourteen to eighteen inches. I lost track of the numbers of fish but my gut instinct tells me we caught very close to a hundred brown trout between us in about three hours time. It was the most incredible trout fishing I've ever experienced.

In the process of catching all those fish I went through about a dozen and a half Elk Hair Caddis flies

tied with a peacock body. The aggressive fish really tore up those flies but I didn't care because I was having a great time. Obviously I had not learned the trick to improve the durability of the peacock body that I'm going to share with you in the next few minutes. Gretchen and I had learned it though when we encountered a similar fishing event several years ago on the Yellowstone River. That evening I went through two flies only because I lost one to a tree that somehow wandered into my backcast. Those darned trees and bushes can sure be inconsiderate sometimes! I must have caught about thirty fish on that second fly but it was still in good enough condition to produce several fish the following evening until a bush decided it wanted the fly more than I did.

Like a lot of flies we tie, Gretchen and I have changed the ole Elk Hair Caddis a bit. Today we tie it on a curved shank hook and have added a "hot spot tag" to the overall recipe. We tie it in a range of sizes from four to twenty two and vary the color to match the natural insect. Of course, I always have a few in my fly box with the peacock body. I guess you could say I've had a love affair with peacock and the curved shank hook for quite a few years. I sure hope Gretchen never finds out! Anyway let's tie this fly and learn how to make a really durable peacock/hackle body.

Peacock Elk Hair Caddis

Hook:	Size 4 to 22, curved shank
Thread:	Lime, color of choice
Tag:	Lime thread, Aqua Flex
Body:	Peacock herl
Hackle:	Grizzly, color of choice
Wing:	Elk body hair
Head:	Trimmed elk hair

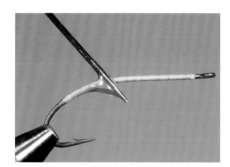

Step 1: Place the hook in the vise, wrap a thread base from the eye to a position even with the end of the barb, and return to the starting point. Whip-finish the thread and trim it from the hook. Apply a coating of Aqua Flex (epoxy, nail polish, etc.) and place the hook in a rotary dryer to allow the glue to set up. If you skip this step it won't take very many fish for you to discover why we need to protect the tag.

Step 2: Remove the now dry, thread-covered hook from the turning wheel and place it back in the vise. Tie the thread back on the hook just behind the eye. Remove the fuzzy material from the base of the stem of a grizzly saddle hackle and tie it to the hook with the feather pointing forward. Select several peacock herls and tie them to the hook by their tips with the base ends pointing forward. Pull the thread forward and grasp it along with the hackle and peacock herl. Rotate the vise several turns constructing a strand of peacock chenille with the hackle imbedded in it.

Step 3: Bring the hackle/peacock chenille perpendicular with the shank and rotate the vise applying the body/hackle from the front to the back of the hook. When you reach the position directly above the hook point tie off the herl/hackle then trim the waste ends.

Step 4: Cover the trimmed ends with several thread wraps then rotate the vise to advance the thread forward over the body. Leave the thread hanging directly behind the eye in preparation of the next step. I find zigzagging the thread while rotating the vise keeps it from mashing down most of the hackle fibers however the more bedraggled the fly appears, the better it seems to attract fish.

Step 5: Select, clean, and stack a clump of elk body hair. Tie it to the shank forming a wing that extends to the rear Trude style ending even with the bend of the hook.

Step 6: Trim the waste ends of hair to form the head. Apply a whip-finish using your preferred technique, you know what I'd like you to do. Coat the thread with Aqua Head to finish the fly. Don't forget to put a dab on the body, tie-off point at the back of the hook.

Abel Quality Products

Steve and Gina Abel founded their company in 1977 to produce precision-milled aerospace and medical parts. In 1987 they used the same technology to begin making fly-fishing reels. Since that first reel the company has evolved into five reel styles with thirty-five different models. Following the Abel Mission Statement (To design and build the best, most dependable gear in the world and give world class customer service.) the company has expanded into all facets of fly-fishing and fly-tying.

Introduced in 1999, the Abel Supreme fly-tying vise is magnificent in appearance and a delight to use. The smooth action of the true rotary head is machined from solid brass and copper. The jaws are stainless steel heat-treated and are easily positioned for "on axis rotation" by aligning the hook shank with the center of the rotation arm. The Supreme and its new cousin the Abel Aluminum Vise hold a wide range of hook sizes from size 28 to 12/0. The new Aluminum Vise is available in a range of anodized colors as illustrated in the photograph. I especially appreciate the machined holes in the pedestal base. They were originally designed for drying flies placed on toothpicks but I found they were also very handy for holding extra bobbins and other tools.

The silky-smooth rotation and the incredible hook holding ability are the first things I immediately noticed about the Abel Supreme as I started construction of our first fly, the Bubble Dancer.

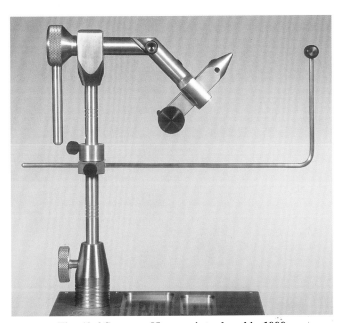

The Abel Supreme Vise was introduced in 1999.

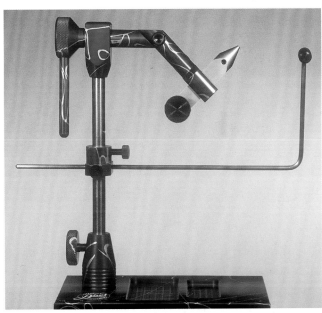

The new Aluminum Vise is available in a range of anodized colors.

Bubble Dancer

When Chris Mihulka sent us this fly for the *Fly Pattern Encyclopedia* Gretchen immediately noticed the appeal and simplicity. She set it aside so we could discuss it further but a move from Delta, Colorado to her hometown in Boise, Idaho got in the way. A couple of years passed until the other day, while digging through a box of fly tying materials, she ran across the container it was in along with her note to me. So long story short, I read her thoughts (a bit late for sure) and agreed, the fly looked like it had great potential for use in salt or freshwater environments. In fact it was very similar to a streamer pattern we often tie for steelhead in our part of the world, The Harvester introduced to us by Bill Marts at the Blue Dun Fly Shop in Spokane, Washington (see the Renzetti Chapter). I also didn't miss the fact this fly was literally made for rotary tying techniques. I'm sure you'll agree when you see how easy it is to tie on an Abel Supreme Vise.

Bubble Dancer

Hook:	Size 2/0 to 10, salt or freshwater style
Thread:	Red or color of choice
Weed guard:	Hard mono, optional
Tail:	Pearl Krystal Flash and orange rubber leg material
Body:	Chartreuse and orange marabou, wrapped in two segments
Eyes:	Dumbbell, color of choice, black pupils
Head:	Thread, Aqua Flex

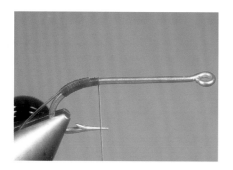

Step 1: Place a hook in the vise and apply a short thread base at the end of the hook shank. Select a section of twenty-five-pound mono and tie it to the end of the shank wrapping part way down into the hook bend. Leave the thread hanging at the end of the shank in preparation for the next step. Notice I temporarily stored the monofilament strand in the slot between the vise jaws. Also, I completed this step and the next using stationary tying techniques rather than rotary.

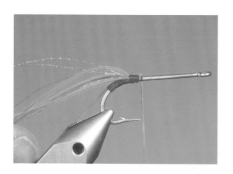

Step 2: Select a couple of strands of pearl Krystal Flash, fold them in half, and cut the material to form four segments. Tie them to the shank as a tail accent. Top them with several strands of orange rubber leg or silicon material to complete the tail. I like the Krystal Flash to be a little longer than the rubber leg material.

Step 3: Prepare a chartreuse marabou feather by stripping the short, fuzzy fibers from the base of the stem. Tie the stripped stem to the underside of the hook and trim off the wasted end. Temporarily store the thread on the bobbin rest. Grasp the marabou feather by its tip, rotate the vise a couple of turns, and tie off the feather on top of the shank. Do not trim off the waste end. Instead pull it back and place a couple of thread wraps to force it to stay back with the rest of the collar.

Step 4: Repeat the process outlined in the previous step with an orange marabou feather placing it in front of the chartreuse. Note: This fly is effective in a wide range of color combinations so let your imagination be your guide.

Step 5: Tie the dumbbell eyes to the hook in front of the orange marabou using several figure-eight wraps. Apply a whip finish, trim off the thread, and set the bobbin aside for the moment. I like to further anchor the eyes with a drop of QuickTite brush-on super glue.

Step 6: Reattach the thread just behind the hook eye, trim the waste end, and retrieve the mono that is stored in the jaw slot. Pull it forward and tie it to the underside of the shank with several tight thread turns. Cut off the excess mono, apply a whip-finish, and trim the thread from the hook. Apply a coating of Aqua Flex to complete the fly. Place it on a turning wheel to set up and dry.

Black John

This is another fly from our book, the *Fly Pattern Encyclopedia* sent to us by Len Elzie. I'll never forget the warm, spring day I opened the package from him. The last thing I wanted to do was work on the book and his fly tipped me over the edge. The Black John was screaming to me, PIKE! PIKE! I understand that Len had sent the fly intended for use in salt water but it didn't take me long to duplicate it several times using freshwater hooks, grab Gretchen and Dubbin, and drive to Crawford Reservoir not far from our home (at that time in Delta, Colorado).

The pike loved the fly from the first cast and it immediately found a permanent spot in our personal fly boxes. Today we tie it in a range of sizes and colors. The small mouth bass in the Snake River a few miles south of our home in Boise, Idaho seem to think it looks a lot like a crawfish when we dead drift it through likely holding water. The brown trout in the Boise River in one of the downtown parks really go for it when stripped across the current. The bluegills in a local pond like it with a black tail accented by a white marabou collar and a palmered body hackle colored white, orange, or brown.

Best of all for my purposes here, it is great for rotary tying. Wait till you see how fast I (and you) can construct the body with a palmered hackle all in one step. This time I'll be placing the thread on the bobbin rest and using the rib to tie off the body/hackle.

Chapter 7: Abel Quality Products

Black John

Hook:	Size 2/0 to 12, salt or freshwater
Thread:	Orange or color of choice
Eyes:	Dumbbell, color to match the body
Rib:	Silver wire or tinsel
Tail:	Black rabbit strip
Back hackle:	Black marabou, pearl Krystal Flash
Body:	Black chenille
Body hackle:	Black, palmered
Head:	Thread

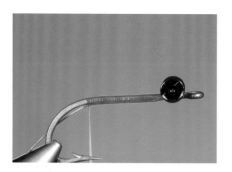

Step 1: Place the hook in the vise and wrap a short thread base just behind the hook eye. Bind the dumbbell eyes to the hook making certain to leave space for constructing the head later. Place a drop of QuickTite super glue to further anchor them. Attach the rib material on the underside of the hook while wrapping the thread to the end of the shank. Place the rib in the jaw slot to keep it out of the way for the time being. Notice I have the rib positioned on the off side of the hook and through the jaw slot. By placing it this way I can use rotary tying procedures to bind it to the hook.

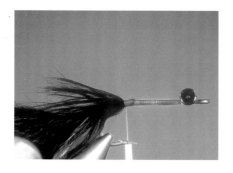

Step 2: Select a piece of rabbit strip with the hide portion equal to the complete hook. Tie it on the end of the shank to form a tail. I've found using a single-edge razor blade to cut the rabbit strip rather than employing scissors keeps to a minimum those awful little tufts of fur from floating around my tying area. I can guarantee you they will get to be a real problem if you tie enough rabbit-strip flies.

Step 3: Strip the short, fuzzy fibers from the base of a marabou stem and tie it to the underside of the shank. Place the thread temporarily in the bobbin rest. Grasp the tip of the feather and rotate the vise to wind it on the hook. Retrieve the bobbin and tie off the feather. Pull its tip back and wrap over the base of the collar to force it to stay back. Tie several strands of pearl Krystal Flash to the hook and position them around the shank so they accent the marabou collar. Wrap the thread forward stopping behind the eyes.

Step 4: Prepare a black hackle feather by stripping the fuzzy fibers from the base of the stem and tie it to the underside of the hook directly behind the eyes. Wrap the thread in front of the eyes and tie on a piece of black chenille. Place the thread in the bobbin holder for the moment.

Step 5: Grasp the chenille and place a figure-eight wrap around the eyes by rotating the hook. Next grab the feather, hold it and the chenille together in the right thumb/forefinger. Rotate the vise while wrapping the chenille/feather to the back of the hook.

Step 6: Finish wrapping the body/hackle, tie it off with the rib, and trim the waste material. Continue rotating the vise to wind the rib forward to the hook eye. Retrieve the thread from the bobbin rest, tie off the rib, trim away the excess, and execute a whip-finish to complete the fly. Apply a coating of Aqua Head to the thread wraps.

Bloody Green Sparkle

During a telephone conversation with my good friend Bob Lay, who at that time lived in Fort Lauderdale, Florida, I happened to mention a product that was new to me. I explained it to him as being a yarn with sparkling tassels sticking out in every direction. He asked if I had the color red and I sure did. One thing led to another and he ended up asking me to tie him a few wounded baitfish patterns to use on a fishing trip for baby tarpon. I tied him a half dozen, mailed them the next day, and waited to hear if they were any good. I waited! And waited! Finally in desperation I called him to find out the results of his trip and to learn how the flies had worked. He acted like he had never gotten them while I kind of mumbled "bad words" under my breath.

He let me hang for a few moments and started chuckling. Darn him! He had suckered me again! He then gave the "rest of the story" as Paul Harvey would say.

It seems the baby tarpon wouldn't leave the fly alone and he had one of his best tarpon trips ending the day giving the remaining flies to the guide as samples to later copy. I've since shared the concept with several fly-fishing club members who found it worked for them. The fly is new enough I've not had the chance to test it in our local Idaho waters but have every confidence it will prove attractive to freshwater fish as well. By the time you are reading these pages I will have had a year of testing under my belt. We'll see what the results may be.

Bloody Green Sparkle

Hook:	Size 3/0 to 6, salt or fresh water
Thread:	Red
Tag:	Red Body Brite
Tail:	Four green cape feathers, splayed
Hackle:	Two folded green feathers, tied as a collar
Hackle accent:	Red Body Brite mixed with the hackle
Eyes:	Dumbbell
Head:	Red Body Brite

Step 1: Place the hook in the vise, apply a thread base that starts at the eye, and stops even with the point. Select a six-inch section of red Body Brite, tie it to the underside of the hook wrapping down into the bend, and returning to the starting point. Wrap a fairly long tag dressing the flashy fibers back after each turn. It is easier to accomplish this step using stationary tying techniques. Tie it off above the hook point, trim off the excess, and set it aside to use in a future step.

Step 2: Select four grizzly, dyed green hackle feathers, pair them, and tie them to the hook so they form a splayed tail. Trim off the waste ends.

Step 3: Note: I've changed to the new Abel Aluminum Vise; it also really holds a hook well. Select two grizzly, dyed green hackle feathers and fold the fibers in preparation for wrapping a wet-style collar. Tie them to the hook by their tips and trim the waste ends. Tie on a segment of red Body Brite at least as long as the hackle feathers and trim the waste end. Wrap the thread forward about half way to the hook eye.

Step 4: Separate the two feathers and sandwich the Body Brite between them. Rotate the vise enough turns to wrap a green hackle collar with a red sparkle core. Tie off the feathers and Body Brite. Trim off the waste ends.

Step 5: Tie on the dumbbell eyes directly in front of the hackle collar. I used several figure-eight wraps to bind them in place. Anchor the eyes further by placing a drop of QuickTite super glue between them. Let it dry before continuing or you could end up gluing your fingers together like I just did. Darn, that's embarrassing!

Step 6: Tie a section of red Body Brite on the shank behind the dumb bell eyes and advance the thread forward to the hook eye. Wrap a couple of turns behind the eyes, figure-eight around them, and wind the Body Brite forward to finish the head. Tie off the material and trim the excess. Apply a whip-finish followed with a coat of Aqua Head to complete the fly.

Tarpon Tamer

For Gretchen and me fly tying falls into categories based on expectation/purpose. Production tying is a way we make a portion of our income. Therefore speed and quality are major considerations at those times. When we are teaching a class speed is not the issue, clarity of the message is our top priority. When we tie to relax, often just constructing something different from what we had been tying through the day fills the bill. That's how Gretchen created the Tarpon Tamer. She was looking for a little escape from an order of Lime Trude flies we were tying for a fly shop in Montana and a box of materials from Rocky Mountain Dubbing UPS delivered that day was sitting on the floor next to her work station. Part of the contents from that box went on a hook along with other available materials. When she showed the completed "relaxation fly" to me I though it looked good and suggested we put it in the book we were writing. At the time it seemed like a good idea and I called it the Green Tarpon.

Let's fast-forward a few weeks as I'm leaving home to catch a plane to Florida to go on my first tarpon-fishing trip. I was quite excited because all my life I had fished for freshwater species with an emphasis on trout, I had never landed any fish that was darned near as big as me. Now I was getting that opportunity.

When I opened my suitcase in the motel at Big Pine Key, Florida I found six of the green tarpon flies Gretchen had slipped in as a surprise. The next day I got shots at seven fish and four of them ate the fly. Each time I raised my rod tip to set the hook I lost the fish. The guide explained (very patiently) I needed to yank on the rod very hard because the tarpon had a mouth like a cement building block. I never did land a fish in the three days I was in Florida just because I couldn't get away from the trout hook-set ingrained in my brain from forty-five years fishing in fresh water.

When I returned home Gretchen asked how the flies had worked and told her they attracted the fish but I just couldn't tame them. The name stuck and the fly became the Tarpon Tamer just as a reminder to me of a time when I had to eat "humble pie" proving I wasn't the expert in all aspects of fly-fishing I thought I was! Oh well, humble pie is a great motivator and it has pushed me to learn a lot about tarpon fishing since that first trip.

Tarpon Tamer

Hook:	Size 3/0 to 2, saltwater
Thread:	Fluorescent green
Tail:	Chartreuse bucktail, green Tiewell flash
Tail flank:	Green hackle
Collar:	Chartreuse neck hackle
Eyes:	Dumbbell, stick-on, gold/black
Snout:	Tying thread coated with Aqua Flex

Step 1: Place the hook in the vise and apply a short thread base at the back of the hook shank. Select a clump of chartreuse bucktail and tie it to the hook as a tail about twice as long as the shank. Top the tail with several strands of green Tiewell Flash that are slightly longer than the tail.

Step 2: Pluck two feathers from a cape dyed dark green. Tie one to the near side of the tail and the other to the far side. Adjust their length so they are a bit shorter than the bucktail. Trim off the waste ends. Up to this point I've applied the materials using stationary tying techniques.

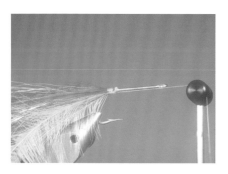

Step 3: Select two strung neck hackles dyed chartreuse. Fold the fibers on each and tie them to the hook by their tips. Place the thread on the bobbin rest.

Step 4: Hold the feather with the right forefinger/thumb and rotate the vise with the left hand to construct the collar. Tie off the feathers and trim their waste ends. Place several thread wraps tight against the hackle to force the fibers back collar style.

Step 5: Tie on the dumbbell eyes directly in front of the collar. I used several figure-eight wraps to firmly anchor them then followed that with a drop of QuickTite super glue.

Step 6: Build a tapered snout, whip-finish just behind the hook eye, and trim off the thread. Attach the stick-on eyes then coat the whole assembly (eyes and snout) with Aqua Flex. Place the fly in a turner to dry. Apply a second coat of Aqua Flex if it is needed.

Beatty's Brainstorm

For the last ten years or so I've had the "perfect" vise formulating in my mind's eye. I've redesigned it numerous times as new ideas would come to the fore. I wanted it be several vises in one, true rotary as well as full rotation with a couple of other functions thrown in for good measure. I've shared the idea with several machinists and a couple of vise manufacturers but really didn't get as far down the road as I wanted. Ron Abby did modify a couple of his Barracuda vises for Gretchen and me coming close to my dream but not quite all the way. The angle of the jaws was not quite what I needed and the head didn't tilt up or down but it did have one of the features no other vise had. I'll share it with you when I tie one of the flies later in this chapter.

I had just about given up on ever seeing my idea actually make the giant leap from thought waves to hard reality until I asked fellow fly-fisher/friend/contractor Jeff Smith to give me a hand knocking out a wall in the house to accommodate a room remodel. After the first day on the job that comprised of the demolition portion, the slower, less dirty part of the project took over. Jeff and I had more time to talk while working. Of course the conversation eventually turned to one of our favorite subjects—fly-tying. I told him about my dream vise and the frustration I encountered trying to bring it to reality. Over lunch on the project's third day the paper tablet came out and rough drawings developed from a four-hour brainstorming session. The remodel project went on temporary hold while we did something much more important—design a vise.

Please understand, Jeff and I are not machinists and the only tools we had to work with were a hacksaw, drill, and bastard file. That day we lashed a very rough prototype together from a spare Danvise, a couple pieces or wood, and a hose clamp. It incorporated all of my ideas but the wood/hose clamp assembly just wouldn't stay together long enough for us to tie a complete fly.

After thinking about it overnight Jeff felt he could accomplish what I wanted by using two Danvises to make one Beatty vise. I sent him home that Friday night

with six Danvises. He sawed, drilled, and filed three very crude prototype vises that incorporated every function I wanted. Yes, the vise you see here looks like a monster but as I use it on the next few flies you will get an idea how some of the features help the fly tier complete maneuvers never before possible with a traditional rotary or full-rotation vise. To be sure, this book is about

The protype vise is a bit cumbersome but it incorporates ALL of the functions I wanted in a vise.

Tilting the head of the vise changes it from a true-rotary tool to a full-rotation unit.

tying flies using the rotating features of a vise but the tool can also be used to position the hook in such a way to help the tier more easily construct a pattern.

Oh yeah! Some of you may be wondering about the

remodel job. It did eventually reach completion but took about a week longer than we had anticipated. However, I had a vise in hand that had only been a dream up to that time. I share it with all of you: machinists, vise makers, and fly tiers. Maybe someone out there will build a vise based on my ideas that has sleek, clean lines with the same functionality; only time will tell. I'll place a postscript at the end of this chapter if such a vise becomes a reality while I'm working on this book.

The jaws rotate a full 360 degrees to place the hook in positions never before possible.

Green Butt Spey

As I recall I first became aware of Spey flies sometime in the mid 80s when I lived in north Idaho and often fished for steelhead on the Clearwater River. Fellow fly-fishers from the North Idaho Fly Casters FFF club introduced me to the fly with the creepy, crawly action named after a river in Scotland. When Gretchen and I moved to Montana our trips to the Clearwater River were sporadic at best and some years we just didn't find the time to make the long drive at all. Gradually my collection of Spey flies dwindled and died. The few times I had the opportunity to go steelhead fishing I tied standard flies like the Green Butt Skunk or borrowed patterns from a friend.

Let's fast forward in time to our return home to Boise, Idaho in 2002. That was the same year John Shewey's great book by Frank Amato Publications, Inc. *Spey Flies & Dee Flies: Their History & Construction* found its way under the Christmas tree in the Beatty household with my name on it. During the last few days of that year John's book rekindled a flame in me that had long since been extinguished. I tied more Spey flies in a few days than I had in my whole life. I had to "make do" regarding materials with whatever I had available. The pickings were darned sparse

to say the least. I didn't have a good heron substitute but found pheasant rump worked fairly well. I was out of teal but had lots of mallard flank feathers. In other words, like a lot of other fly tiers, I employed what I had.

The flies looked good enough to go fishing and that's just what I did. Each winter the Idaho Fish and Game Department truck in steelhead from out of town and release them in the Boise River to give anglers unable to travel a chance to catch one. I had a lot of fun with those fish and my "make do" Spey flies. Since then my supply of materials has exploded and I have whatever I need to tie just about any Spey fly. I've also made an interesting discovery. The fish don't seem to be any more impressed with the fancy flies I tied with exotic materials than they do with Spey flies constructed from plain old pheasant. Go figure!

Starting here I'm tying with the prototype vise. Not only will I use regular rotary-tying techniques but I will also use the many different adjustments available to me to position the fly so it is easier to access different parts of the hook. I've only tied on this prototype for a few months and I'm constantly amazed at how much easier all aspects of tying have become. Let's see what you think of it.

Green Butt Spey Materials

Hook:	Size 2/0 to 4, salmon type hook
Thread:	White, green, and black
Tag:	Silver oval tinsel, green thread
Tail:	Red Amherst pheasant crest feather
Body:	Black yarn
Rib:	Silver oval tinsel
Hackle:	Pheasant rump feather
Collar:	Mallard flank feather
Wing:	White Icelandic wool
Head:	Black thread

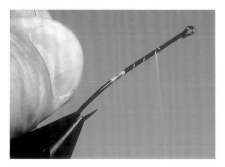

Step 1: Place the hook in the vise and attach white tying thread slightly forward of the hook point using four turns. Trim the waste end then attach silver tinsel to the under side of the hook shank. Bind it to the hook to a position half way between the point and the barb. Temporarily advance the thread forward on the hook shank to get it out of the way. This vise has the ability to rotate the whole vise OR the jaws independent of each other. Here I rotated the jaws (not the vise) a half turn so I could more easily access the back of the hook to place the first of five tinsel turns required to construct the tip of the tag.

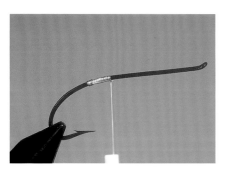

Step 2: Construct a five-turn tinsel application, unwrap the white thread stored forward on the shank, tie off the material, and return the jaws to their standard position. Bind the tinsel to the underside of the hook while advancing the thread back to its starting position. Trim off the waste ends of the tinsel.

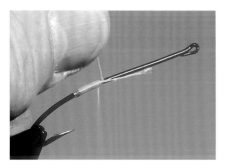

Step 3: Gretchen and I prefer size A un-waxed thread instead of single strand floss and that's what I used to construct the tag on this fly. Note again that I repositioned the jaws so I could get better access to the back of the hook.

Step 4: Select a red crest feather from an Amherst pheasant and tie it to the hook to form the tail. Do not trim off the waste end. Tie a segment of silver, oval tinsel on the under side of the hook advancing the thread forward anchoring the two materials to the shank. Stop at the looped eye platform and trim away the excess of each.

Chapter 8: Beatty's Brainstorm

Step 5: Separate a six-inch segment of four-strand yarn into single units. Tie one of them to the top of the hook while wrapping back to meet the tail. Select a pheasant rump feather, stroke the fibers back along the stem, and fold them. Tie this feather to the bottom of the hook shank by its tip. Trim any excess at the looped eye platform. Whip-finish the white thread then attach the black. Place it in the bobbin rest, grasp the black yarn, and rotate the vise to apply the body.

Step 6: Tie off the yarn and trim the waste end. Again place the thread in the bobbin rest. Bring the pheasant feather and the rib tight together. Hold them at about a forty-five-degree angle and rotate the vise to apply the feather/rib all at the same time. I found anchoring the two in a hackle pliers helped me maintain control of them.

Step 7: Tie off the feather/rib then trim the waste ends. Select a mallard flank feather and strip the fibers from one side of the stem. Tie it on the hook by its tip, place the thread in the bobbin rest, and rotate the vise to wrap the collar. Retrieve the thread from the bobbin rest, tie it off, and trim the waste end. The collar fibers tend to marry together. I find stroking them with a mustache comb breaks them apart and shapes the collar around the hook.

Step 8: Trim a small bundle of white Icelandic wool from the pelt and tie it to the hook to form a wing long enough to reach the end of the tail. Trim the waste end, build a head, whip-finish the thread, and trim it from the hook. I like to add a couple of coats of Aqua Tuff to finish the fly with a clear, glossy head.

Quick'n EZY Adams

I first learned about swept back hackle fiber wings in the late 80s on a trip to Europe. The people who showed me the style referred to them as Wonder Wings. They were tied using the swept-back fibers from two hackle feathers. The swept-back fibers and feather stem were bound to the hook, stood up, and when the waste ends were trimmed the wing just magically appeared.

I thought they were beautiful and incorporated them in my fly patterns when I returned from my European jaunt. The first time I fished them I learned why they were not particularly popular here in the US. The stiff stem in the center of the wing caused the fly to "propeller" during the casting process resulting in a badly twisted leader. I temporarily retired the wing style with the promise to myself to find a fix for the twisted leader syndrome as soon as I could.

The Quick'n EZY got its start quite by accident. I was fishing a "walk-in section" of the Coeur 'd Alene River in north Idaho one sunny day. I was having a great time catching a good number of nice cutthroat trout on a standard Adams dry fly. In fact that fly was the only thing the fish would look at that day. Things started to go wrong when I lost a fly to a willow that wandered into my backcast and was in the process of selecting another Adams from my fly box. This guy named Murphy ran out of the brush, grabbed my open fly box, and threw it (with all my Adams patterns) into the water. As quickly as he appeared Murphy vaporized into thin air leaving me many miles from tying any replacements flies (or so I

By clipping out a section of the stems, I transformed the stiff wings into a softer, loop style eliminating the leader twist while still maintaining a similar profile.

thought). I tried a few other patterns hoping something would prove attractive to the trout but they had gotten a sudden case of lockjaw. I was sitting on the riverbank thinking about my situation when I remembered a small collection of tying materials I carry in a zip-lock bag in my fishing vest. It didn't contain much—several feathers (brown, grizzly and dun), thread, hooks, and dubbing—just enough to tie a nymph or two in an emergency. Using my hemostats and nippers I constructed a rough version of what you see here. That single fly saved the day for me. Yes it did cause my leader to twist but I discovered I could transform it into a looped wing by clipping out a section of the stem next to the hook shank with my leader nippers to eliminate the problem. From that day forward I've used the looped Wonder Wing in place of hackle points on all of my personal flies however it did take several months to develop the tying method I'll demonstrate in next few paragraphs. The wing style has served me well over the years. I guess I should thank Murphy for throwing my flies in the water that day but for some reason he has never shown his face again. Maybe that's because I'm a lot more careful with my open fly boxes when I'm close to the water than I was that day.

In the tying steps I'll illustrate a "back and forth" hackling technique you may find interesting. Also, I'm using orange thread so you can see the contrast between the materials and the thread, however I normally use a thread color to match the body of the insect I'm trying to imitate.

Quick'n EZY Adams

Hook:	Size 8 to 24, dry fly
Thread:	Orange or color to match insect
Tail:	Hackle fibers, grizzly/brown mix
Wings:	Looped hackle fibers
Body:	Gray dubbing or match the insect
Hackle:	Grizzly/brown mix
Head:	Thread

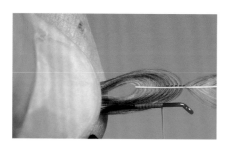

Step 1: Place the hook in the vise and lay down the thread base that starts at the one-fourth position travels to the center of the shank and back to the starting point. Select two large, grizzly feathers from a rooster cape. Place them so the natural curve slopes away from each other and trim off the large end of the stem (about one-third of the complete feather length). Keep the trimmed stems even with each other with the tips pointing to the right. Hold the feathers in the right hand with about an inch of the butt ends exposed and stroke back the fibers on segments of stem each two-thirds of the hook shank in length.

Step 2: Tie this unit to the hook shank in the center of the stems (the part that is two-thirds the length of the shank) using three snug but not tight thread wraps. Do not loose control of the fiber ends in the left hand.

Step 3: Pull on the feather tips with the right hand allowing the fibers/stems to slip out from under the three snug thread turns. Do not pull too hard with the right hand or the whole swept back unit will jump out from under the thread. Pull on the bobbin with the right hand to tighten the thread then place a couple tight wraps to further anchor the wing assembly in place. During this process, never loose control of the fibers in the left hand. This eliminates the need for trimming a piece of stem from each wing as indicated in Picture Four and is one of the modifications in the evolution of the pattern.

Step 4: Release the fibers captured in the left hand. Somewhere in that mess is the tail. It is up to the tier to determine the fibers that are too short or too long to form a properly proportioned tail and get rid of them.

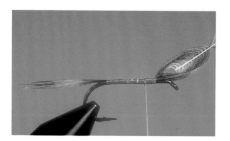

Step 5: The fibers remaining that are the correct length form the first half of the tail. I like a tail about as long as the complete hook. Wrap the thread forward to a position near the base of the wings.

Step 6: An Adams tail is usually a mix of grizzly and brown hackle fibers however finding good tailing fibers in our modern day, genetic capes can be a problem. I have found a small bundle of stacked squirrel tail to be an excellent substitute for hackle fibers and that's what I'm using here.

Step 7: Tie the bundle of squirrel tail fibers on top of the grizzly remaining for Step five. Trim off the waste ends near the base of the wings.

Step 8: Pull the wing assembly up straight and wrap a thread dam in front to force it to remain up right. Pull the feather unit apart to form two wings, then trim the waste ends. Turn the jaws (not the vise) a quarter turn so the hook eye is pointing away giving a better view of the wings. Crisscross wrap between the wings to provide better definition and separation.

Step 9: Apply dubbing to the thread and construct a body on the back two-thirds of the shank. Select brown and grizzly hackle feathers, prepare them by stripping the fuzzy fibers from the base of the stem, and tie them to the hook - one behind the wings and the other near the hook eye. Apply more dubbing to the thread and wrap over the front one-third of the hook shank.

Step 10: Place the brown hackle in the material keeper. Grasp the grizzly feather and the thread with the right hand and rotate the vise to apply the hackle traveling back to meet the brown hackle.

Step 11: Upon reaching the brown hackle anchor the grizzly with a couple of thread turns. Recover the brown feather from the material keeper and bring it in-line with the thread. Again, rotate the vise to wrap the brown hackle forward.

Step 12: After reaching the hook eye tie off the brown feather and trim the waste end. Apply a whip-finish, clip the thread from the hook, and apply a coating of Aqua Head. Trim the grizzly feather and apply a drop of Aqua Head at that position to complete the fly. Why did I hackle in this manner? It is more durable because the feathers cross over each other during the tying process. It's just another option for you, the fly tier.

Chapter 8: Beatty's Brainstorm

The Quick'n EZY Parachute (PMD)

If you've every watched a mayfly dun hatch you will understand why I like my parachute patterns with divided wings. The emerging insect first appears in my world as a small lump floating in/on the water's surface. As the emergence continues its wings start unfolding. At first they are crumpled but separated and as they dry they become straight and divided. When the wings are completely dry they come together and the mayfly leaves the water. I think the fish learn the emerging dun is unable to fly when its wings are divided and will key on that fact. I find this especially true in slow water like a spring creek where the fish have plenty of time to study its prey. Obviously, this idea has less merit in many freestone streams where the fish has limited time to study its intended meal.

Does the divided wing make a difference? I really don't know but I'm sure of one thing, I catch a heck of a lot of fish on a divided wing parachute. One could argue that's because ninety percent of the time when I'm fishing a parachute pattern it has divided wings. I believe the fish just like that wing style because they recognize it as a helpless insect unable to escape. Whichever side of the fence you believe doesn't really make any difference. My purpose here is not to convince you one of my "hair-brained theories" has value; instead I want to share with you a way of tying a parachute (using a feature of the vise) that I think is a bit innovative.

Before I tie the fly I want to comment that the swept-back wing style on a parachute took me the better part of five years to figure out. Tying the wing was no big deal but strengthening the hackle fibers so they would support a parachute hackle was another thing indeed. I tried monofilament and wire hidden in the base of the wings but was never really happy with them. Finally I stumbled on the technique I'll share with you in the next few minutes.

Again, I'm using orange thread to provide contrast between it and the tying materials. Normally I would use tan thread on a PMD Parachute or a color that matches the insect for other mayfly species.

Quick'n EZY Parachute (PMD)

Hook:	Size 8 to 22, dry fly
Thread:	Tan, color to match the insect
Tail:	Hackle fibers
Wings:	Looped hackle fibers
Body:	Dubbing to match the insect
Hackle:	Color to match the insect

Step 1: Place the hook in the vise and lay down the thread base that starts at the one-fourth position travels to the center of the shank and back to the starting point. Select two large, ginger feathers from a rooster cape. Place them so the natural curve slopes away from each other and trim off the large end of the stem. Keep the trimmed stems even with each other and the tips pointing to the right. Hold the feathers in the right hand with about an inch of the butt ends exposed and stroke back the fibers on segments of stem each two-thirds of the hook shank in length. Tie this unit to the hook in the center of the stems (the part that is two-thirds the length of the shank) using three snug but not tight thread wraps. Do not lose control of the fiber ends in the left hand.

Step 2: Pull on the feather tips with the right hand allowing the fibers/stems to slip out from under the three snug thread turns. Do not pull too hard with the right hand or the whole swept back unit will jump out from under the thread. Pull on the bobbin with the right hand to tighten the thread then place a couple tight wraps to further anchor the wing assembly in place. During this process, never lose control of the fibers in the left hand.

Step 3: Release the fibers captured in the left hand. Somewhere in that mess is the tail. It is up to the tier to determine the fibers that are too short or too long to form a properly proportioned tail and get rid of them. Bind the remaining fibers to the shank forming a tail about as long as the complete hook. Up to this point the process is identical to a standard Quick 'n EZY.

Step 4: Stand up the wing assembly with a thread dam tight in front of the fibers. At this point I want to construct a thread-based, hackle platform over the wing fibers. I find it a lot easier to rotate the vise one-half turn so I don't have to raise my arm to wrap up the post. Wind up the wing (even though I'm wrapping down) to the top of the post area then go straight back to the body (the thread is parallel to the back of the post) and anchor the thread there with several wraps. Wrap up the post in the opposite direct then go straight to the body again and anchor the thread with several wraps. I call the process of going around the wing "pouring cement" and the straight up and down strand of thread "placing rebar." Go through the process one more time ending with the piece of rebar.

Step 5: Separate the wings then trim off the waste feather. Place the waste pieces of feather in a clothespin for use on a future fly. Crisscross between wings forcing them to remain separated. Notice the wraps also form four more pieces of rebar each paralleling the post. Leave the strands of rebar alone for a moment; I'll anchor them in a few minutes.

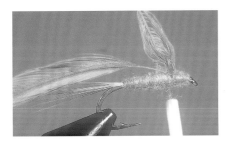

Step 6: Place dubbing on the thread and construct the body up to the back of the wing post. Prepare a hackle feather by stripping the fuzzy material from the end of the stem. Tie it to the hook directly in front of the post. Apply more dubbing to the thread to cover the part of the hook between the post and the eye. Then wrap back to the post ending with the last turn behind it.

Step 7: Rotate the jaws (not the vise) so the wings are parallel with the tying bench surface. Wrap the thread up the post while anchoring the stem and the last four pieces of rebar.

Step 8: Grasp the thread and hackle with the right hand and rotate the vise (not the jaws) to apply the hackle. The thread platform will rotate more or less on axis allowing for a smooth application of the hackle.

Chapter 8: Beatty's Brainstorm

Step 9: Wrap hackle all the way down the post until it meets the body. Anchor the feather with two thread wraps.

Step 10: Trim off the excess feather then place one more turn of thread to tuck the trimmed end under.

Step 11: Use a tool or fingers to place a whip-finish on the base of the post.

Step 12: Trim off the thread and apply a drop of Aqua Head to complete the fly. Often the wings will twist during the hackling process. Don't worry about it; just use your fingers to straighten them out before applying the head cement.

Step 13: I placed a double whip-finish to exaggerate the separation between the bottom of the hackle and the body. When you tie your fly make your whip-finish less noticeable or just pull the thread forward to the hook eye and tie it off there rather than on the post.

Step 14: Rotating the jaws a partial turn throws the fly in an odd position in the picture frame but the different angle shows a good wing profile and the whip-finish on the bottom of the hackle platform/post.

Humpy

The Humpy is one of the more versatile offerings in a trout fisher's bag of tricks. It can represent a large stonefly or a small ant depending on color/size used in its construction. As an example, I like to fish a #16 fluorescent yellow Humpy during a yellow sally hatch because trout seem to find it attractive even though it doesn't look much like the natural insect. Suffice it to say, many fly-fishers use the Humpy for a variety of fishing situations because it is very effective.

With that said, it's also been my experience that many fly-dressers don't have the same enthusiasm for tying the Humpy that they do for fishing it. Why? Because tying the fly is pain in the neck. It's what I call a "creeper." A creeper is a pattern that sneaks forward on the hook shank when the tier is not looking. This situation becomes very evident when the tier discovers there is no room left to wrap the hackle or finish off the head. If the humpys you tie are pulling this dirty trick on you, then read on. Maybe the next few words can help with that problem!

I am changing vises to one that Ron Abby (Dyna-King, Inc.) modified for me several years ago when I talked with him about my "dream vise." He changed a standard Barracuda by adding the rotating handle then modified the existing jaws so they could be rotated in a complete circle separate from the true rotary feature of the vise itself. In fact, this vise came very close to meeting my needs for the perfect vise but the head did not tilt up and down. One of the things Ron's modified vise (or my prototype) really helped me with my tying was the ability to position the fly so I could get a good look at the wing fibers prior to dividing them into separate clumps. The two clumps almost always come out evenly divided when I view the fly directly from behind (or front based on the tier's preference).

A modified Dyna-King Barracuda with a rotating handle was the first change Ron Abby made for me in my quest for the "dream vise."

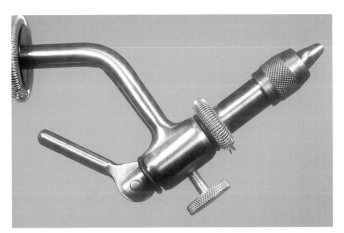

The standard Barracuda jaws would move up and down but did not rotate independently of the vise.

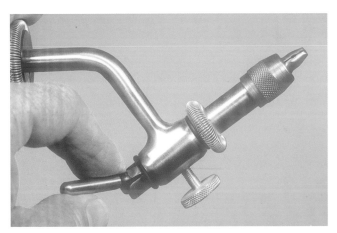

The jaws on the modified vise would move up and down as well as rotate in a complete circle.

Humpy

Hook:	Size 6 to 20, dry fly
Thread:	Yellow, color of choice
Tail:	Moose hair
Wings:	Elk hair
Hump:	Elk or deer hair
Hackle:	Grizzly/brown mix

Step 1: Start the thread base in the middle of the hook shank. Wrap from there to the end of the shank and back to the center of the hook. Cut a clump of moose hair, remove the short fibers and under fur, stack it, and tie on a tail as illustrated that is equal in length to the hook shank. Note the "creeper phenomenon" has started, the trimmed moose tail fibers are slightly forward of the thread. That's why I started the thread in the center of the hook on the illustrated number eight fly. If I were tying a number twenty Humpy, I would start the thread directly above the hook point. To adjust for the "creeper phenomenon" the simple rule is: If your thread is located where you think you want it, then back up two turns or suffer the consequences.

Step 2: Select, clean, and stack a clump of elk hair. Tie on the clump of hair at the one-third point adjusting the length so it is equal to the hook shank. Do not trim the excess material. Instead bind it over the top of the tail fibers and trim it near the end of the hook. This maneuver forms part of the hump making the next step easier. Cover wrap the trimmed ends and leave the thread hanging in the middle of the body area.

Step 3: Select a clump of deer or elk hair and clean the short fibers and under fur. Do not stack the hair. Tie this on the hook by the butt ends in the middle of the body area, wrap to the end of the shank, back to the starting point, and then forward stopping slightly behind the wing material. Note the hair ends are actually slightly forward of the middle of the body and that's where we want them. Remember material creep and adjust your tie in point accordingly. Also, it is a good idea to maintain control of these fibers with the left hand to avoid accidentally mixing them with the tail hair.

Step 4: Pull the clump of hair up and over. The easiest way to tighten the hair fibers in the hump is to press forward with a finger of your left hang (assuming a right handed tier) on the junction point of the tail and hump material. You can pull on the fibers forever and seldom get a smooth, tight hump - push it tight, don't pull it. Tie the fibers off slightly back from the base of the wings. Do not use real tight thread wraps; six should be enough to secure the hair. Trim the excess material. Note the trimmed hump fibers are left fairly long as illustrated.

Step 5: I've rotate the jaws (not the vise) a part of a turn so the hook eye is point away from me giving me clear view of the clump of hair. From this vantage point I can easily determine how much hair should go into each wing post.

Step 6: Crisscross wrap the thread between the divided hair bundles then return the jaws to their original position. Rotate the vise one-half turn so the wings are pointing down. Now I can easily wrap around each wing post without having to raise my arm (aggravating my arthritic shoulder). Wind several thread wraps around the base of each wing. In doing so you should be capturing the trimmed ends from the hump incorporating them into the base of each wing post. Besides anchoring the trimmed hair from the hump this maneuver forces the wings to stand up straight.

Step 7: Prepare a grizzly and brown hackle by stripping the fuzzy fibers from the base of the stem. Tie them to the underside of the hook behind the hair wings. Wrap the thread forward and store it temporarily in the bobbin keeper. Rotate the vise a couple of turns starting the hackle application. It is quite easy to wrap two feathers at the same time if the hand holding the hackle remains stationary and the vise does the turning.

Step 8: Finish wrapping the hackle, retrieve the thread from the bobbin rest, tie off the feathers, and trim them from the hook. Wrap a head, construct a whip-finish, and trim the thread from the hook. I like to complete the fly with a coating of Aqua Flex on the head and the hump. Note that this vise (and my prototype) provides access to the hook from many different directions but also allows the use of rotary tying techniques when I choose to use them.

The Water Walker

In the early 80s Rob Miner, owner of a fly shop I tied for commercially, called me explaining he had a great new fly for me to see. He suggested I stop in his store the next time I was in town. At that time in my life I was a part time fly tier and a full time manager for a large utilities company. I had to do some creative job planning to be at his store then next day as it was forty-five miles from my regular assignment. Now don't any of you get excited about dereliction of duty or some such idea; I really did come up with a reason (excuse) to be that far from my regular duty station. I do admit the reason was pretty flimsy but it did bring me to his store the next day at noon, just in time for my lunch break.

When I walked into his shop Rob grinned and reach for a fly box sitting to the side of the cash register. He pulled a dry fly out of the box and threw it way up in the air. It settled gently on the counter next to a display rack of sunglasses (I don't know why I remember that silly detail but anyway...) positioned perfectly; wings up resting on its hackle tips. He repeated the "pitch it in the air" process several more times with the same results, a perfectly positioned dry fly.

On first glance it looked like a standard Wulff that someone had done a lousy job of applying the hackle. Upon closer inspection I discovered it was a Gray Wulff alright but the hackle was wrapped parachute style around each wing post - a double parachute. He explained that our mutual friend Frank Johnson (owner of a fly shop in Missoula, Montana) had developed the pattern and oh-by-the-way, could you tie fifty dozen for me by next week?

I left the shop wondering just how I would accomplish his request. He gave me a general idea how the fly was tied but hadn't actually constructed one himself. I struggled for the next several days and finally did get the order done. In the process I became pretty darned good at tying a double parachute. I tied the pattern a lot over the next years and got fairly fast constructing it but never as speedy as I wanted. I sure wish I had my prototype vise then; I could have really smoked those flies using it, as you will see in the next few paragraphs as I tie the Water Walker. Please understand I've made some changes from the original tied by Frank Johnson. Watch closely how to construct a hair-winged fly with a slender profile; not something you normally associate with a Wulff style pattern.

Water Walker

Hook:	Size 8 to 20, dry fly
Thread:	Gray, color of choice
Tail:	Deer or elk hair
Wings:	Deer or elk hair
Body:	Gray dubbing, color of choice
Hackle:	Grizzly or dun
Head:	Thread

Step 1: Place the hook in the vise and apply a thread base starting at the one-third position. Wrap it to the end of the shank and half way back to the starting point. Select a clump of deer or elk body hair, clean out the under fur, and even the tips in a stacker. Tie them to the hook as a tail that is as long as the shank and be certain to keep this bundle fairly sparse. Trim away the waste ends and wind the thread back to the one-third position. Leave it there in preparation for the next step.

Step 2: Normally on this style of fly the bundle of hair for a set of wings is twice as big as the tail because each post should equal it (the tail) in size. Select a clump of fibers half as big as required for a regular hair wing application. Clean out the under fur and even the tips in a stacker. Tie them to the hook, tips pointing forward, adjusting their length to equal the tail. Trim off the waste hair and cover wrap the clipped ends to form a smooth under body. Wrap a small thread dam in front of the incomplete wing to force the fibers to stand up. A well-placed thumbnail will also convince the hair to stand up straight.

Step 3: Select another clump of hair that is equal in size to the first, clean out the under fur, and even the tips in a stacker. Tie the fibers to the front of those from Step two making certain they are anchored tight against them. Trim the excess hair from the hook a few at a time.

Step 4: Finish trimming the fibers clipping them in small bundles until they have all been removed. Cover wrap the trimmed ends to construct the front part of the body.

Step 5: Rotate the vise jaws part of a turn to expose a back view of the wing fibers. Separate the bundle into two posts. I like viewing the wings from the back but the concept works equally well from the front, just rotate the jaws in the opposite direction.

Step 6: Crisscross wrap the thread between the two bundles then wind several turns around each to construct two parachute platforms. I like to position the vise jaws at a different angle for the far wing then readjust to accommodate the near. The ability to rotate the jaws AND the vise certainly gives me unlimited positions I can place the fly so I can easily access whatever part of the pattern I wish.

Step 7: Return the vise to the standard position, apply dubbing to the thread then construct the body behind the wings. Prepare and tie on a single, long saddle feather then apply dubbing to the area in front of the wings making certain the last turn is behind them. I like to position this feather close to the near side wing because it is the first to receive the hackle application. Also, I find wrapping the hackle much easier if I spread the wings apart slightly using my finger or scissors. I'll readjust them after I finish wrapping the hackle. The thread should be hanging behind the wings.

Step 8: Rotate the jaws so the near side wing is parallel to the top of the tying table. Grasp the thread and feather together between the thumb and forefinger of the right hand then rotate the vise to apply the hackle. I wrap the feather up the wing post then back down to meet the body. Do not let go of the thread/feather.

Step 9: Reposition the jaws (not the vise) so the off side wing is now parallel with the tying table surface. Now rotate the vise again to start the application of the parachute hackle to the second wing.

Step 10: Wrap up the post and then back down to meet the body. Anchor the hackle to the bottom of the post with two thread turns then trim off the excess feather.

Chapter 8: Beatty's Brainstorm

Step 11: Apply a whip-finish to the base of the off side wing then trim the thread from the hook. Clip off any stray fibers that may have inadvertently been captured by the whip-finish.

Step 12: Press the wings back together so they form a thirty-degree angle. The parachute hackle around each post provides footprints very similar to those of a natural mayfly.

9
Fisker Design

It's kind of funny how things work out. In 1993 Gretchen and I were in Europe at a fly-fishing show where we met Per Nielson from Denmark. During the course of our conversation I gave him one of my cards and invited him to visit us at our home in Bozeman, Montana should he ever end up in our part of the world.

About a year later the phone rang one evening and it was Per. He was in the Missoula airport with two of his friends where he had just learned his host was unable to welcome them into his home. Per wanted to know if he could stay with us in Bozeman and we agreed. Several hours later we had guests, two of whom we had never met. They stayed with us for a couple of weeks spending almost every day fishing the many excellent waters in the area.

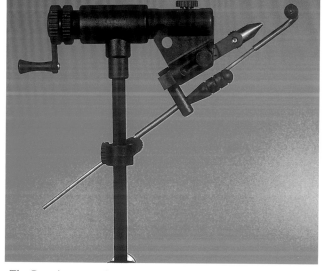

The Danvise was originally known by the Danica name prior to Fisker's sale of the fly box part of his company.

During that time we became best friends and invited them to come back the next year.

The next summer Per again returned and this time his boss, Johnny Fisker, accompanied the group. Johnny spent several days fishing but also spent quite a bit of time with Gretchen and me. We learned he was a distributor/manufacturer of fly-fishing and tying equipment/materials, one of the largest in Europe. He

had started as a college student in 1976 by importing feathers from China and gradually moved into the manufacture of products including Danica fly boxes. Both of us were very familiar with the boxes having a couple of them in our fishing vests filled with flies.

Toward the end of the visit Johnny told us he wanted to share a prototype of a true rotary vise he was preparing to manufacture/distribute around the world. After looking it over he asked, "Would you two distribute it in the USA for me?" We both were stunned but soon reached an agreement sealed with a handshake.

The Danvise you see here is one of many we've sold across the US. It went through a name change several years ago when Johnny sold the Danica Fly Box part of his business. We think it is one of the better true rotary vises priced under $100.00 and use it in much of our day-to-day commercial tying. Like I stated at the start of this piece, "It's kind of funny how things work out." Gretchen and I started a business based on a chance comment at a show in Europe followed by an exchange of business cards. You just never know what interesting twist life will offer!

Goddard Caddis

I well remember an afternoon several years ago. A slight breeze was causing a bit of chop on the water, not a lot, just enough to allow me to stalk fairly close to the fish before making my cast. The Goddard Caddis landed lightly on the water just in front of the cruising fish. A

nose appeared for just a moment and the fly was gone. Feeling the hook point take hold the fish turned and left the country with my reel singing the tune any fly-angler loves to hear. It wasn't long though when concern replaced my exhilaration as the fly line shot through the guides and my backing was disappearing rapidly. Fortunately for me I was fishing in a small lake and the fish did not have a lot of room in which to play. It ran me in circles for several minutes before finally sliding next to my pontoon boat where I promptly released the golden-sided fish.

It was my first carp on a dry fly. I don't know why but up to that time I had not considered carp and dry flies in the same thought but that day changed my mind forever. Today a dry fly is not my go-to solution when I run into a group of carp that seem to have lock jaw but it is one of the list of tricks I employ in the process of figuring out what will attract them. The Goddard Caddis is at the top of the dry fly list.

I also want to note it is not just a dry fly I use for carp but it serves me well for trout and smallmouth bass as well. Gretchen and I have a special spot on the Madison River where it really drives the resident rainbows crazy. Of course that location will have to remain unnamed for now.

My real purpose in this chapter featuring the Danvise is to show all of you how a true-rotary vise really makes spinning and trimming hair a "walk in the park." If you sometimes have trouble with spun hair then the instructions for the next few patterns should really help you improve the appearance of your flies. As some of you probably already know, a good quality spun-hair fly is based on hair distribution and its symmetrical trimming. Let's take a look at a spinning hair technique you've probably not often seen before.

Goddard Caddis

Hook:	Size 8 to 20, dry fly or Stimulator style
Thread:	Lime green
Tag:	Thread
Tail:	Flared & trimmed deer hair
Body:	Spun & trimmed deer hair
Antenna:	Maxima monofilament or hackle stems
Hackle:	Brown

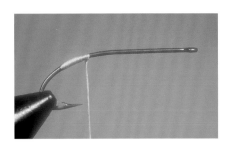

Step 1: Place the hook in the vise and apply a thread base that starts at the end of the hook shank. Wrap the thread down into the hook bend and back to the starting point. Trim off the waste thread end. Note: This step anchors the thread to the hook and at the same time constructs the tag. It also leaves the hook shank bare to help facilitate the spinning process in the next several steps.

Step 2: On this fly the tail actually looks (and is) part of the body however it is constructed by flaring the hair in place rather than spinning it around the hook. Therefore I'm using regular stationary tying techniques to complete the operation. Select a clump of deer hair and remove the under fur. Bind the clump to the end of the shank flaring it on top of the hook. Do not let go of the waste ends but instead keep it under control. Note: This part of the step is so important I used a strip of tape to make sure I didn't lose control of the hair during the photography process. Trim the waste fibers at an angle as illustrated.

Step 3: Notice the angle after making the trim; the tail (really the end of the body) is completed with one clip of the scissors. Advance the thread forward a couple of turns and leave it there for the next step. Advancing the thread gives the next clump of hair room to spin.

Step 4: Select a clump of deer hair and remove the under fur. Bind it to the hook with three snug wraps and trim off the tips. Notice I've angled the clump of hair across the shank on the near side of the hook.

Step 5: Grasp the bobbin with the right hand. Hold it in such a way as to NOT allow the spool to turn while keeping the thread perpendicular to the shank. Personally I like to pinch the spool in the palm of my hand while holding the barrel between my thumb and forefinger.

Step 6: Holding my right hand firm I'm rotating the vise through eighty-percent of a single turn. As the thread is not allowed to feed from the bobbin it is gradually getting shorter and tighter causing the hair to start the spinning process.

Step 7: Finish the last part of that turn and complete another one and one-half rotations of the vise. Notice the hair is almost completely spun around the hook shank.

Step 8: Complete the last one-half turn finishing the hair application. Remember, I had advanced the thread forward a bit in front of the tail material. Use a hair packer to push the spun hair back tight against the tail fibers. Note: I'm sorry it took so long to explain this but what really happens in the blink of an eye in real life takes a bit longer to explain with still photographs and words. Also please note, the hair is evenly distributed around the shank. Why? Because I rotated the vise while holding the bobbin hand firm thus smoothly shortening (and tightening) the thread while each turn evenly increased the pressure on the hair fibers. Inconsistent thread pressure is the reason hand-spun hair is often distributed around the hook unevenly. A true-rotary vise can help solve that problem.

Step 9: From this point you know how to spin hair so apply several more clumps to the hook making certain to cover the back three-fourths of the shank. Don't forget to pack the hair after each application. Whip-finish the thread and temporarily trim it from the hook.

Step 10: Rotate the vise one-half turn so the underside of the hook/hair is facing up. Trim the bottom of the body flat as close to the shank as possible.

Step 11: Rotate the vise back one-fourth turn and position the scissors at a slight angle to the hook shank so the trimmed hair fibers are shorter near the front of the hook and longer at the back. Slowly rotate the vise while trimming hair at the same angle on all sides of the hook. In this illustration I've complete three clips moving the vise a small part of a turn after each snip.

Step 12: Continue trimming the body maintaining the same angle on each snip until the it is complete. Note how easy it is to get an evenly shaped body by rotating the vise while keep the scissors stationary and at the same angle throughout the process.

Step 13: Reattach the tying thread in front of the newly trimmed body. Select two strands of Maxima monofilament, tie them to the front of the hook to serve as antenna, and trim them to length. Select a brown hackle feather and remove the fuzzy material at the base of the stem. Tie this feather to the front of the hook, bring the feather and thread together, and start winding the hackle back to meet the body. Notice the thread is leading the hackle in the process.

Step 14: Upon reaching the body, reverse the direction wrapping the hackle back to the front. Don't forget to move the thread to the front of the hackle before rotating the vise to wind the feather forward. Tie it off at the front of the hook and trim the excess. Apply a whip-finish and trim the waste end of thread followed by a drop of Aqua Head to complete the fly.

Deer Hair Popper

I was once asked to write a magazine piece describing my favorite fish. To the surprise of many, my answer was not one of the more exotic species as might be expected but instead was the crappie. You see, for years I've had this soft spot in my heart for warmwater fish caught from farm ponds and small lakes. I guess this "weakness" in character stems from my first fish on a fly. It was a crappie caught on a bucktail streamer at Mill Creek State Park near Paullina, Iowa more than fifty years ago.

I'll never forget the experience! My casting skills were so bad that getting the fly in the water was challenge number one. After several attempts I did manage to cast the fly about fifteen feet. As I was trying to gather the extra slack, my fly line/leader started to head out into the lake. Long story short, a crappie took pity on me and hung onto the fly much longer than logic tells me it should have. Anyway, it gave me one heck of a good tug taking forever to land—at least that's how my youthful mind remembers the episode.

From that day forward I was hooked on fly-fishing for warmwater fish and not long after I saw an article in *Field & Stream* magazine featuring balsa wood poppers.

I didn't have any balsa wood but figured a piece of a stick from a tree might work and it did after I shaped it a bit with my pocketknife. It didn't take me long to figure out catc[...] [...]ppie on poppers was even more fun than it w[...] on subsurface patterns.

As time [...]ent by I discovered the wonder[...] [...]pun hair. At first it was a magical thing that just kind of happened all by its[...]f[...] some of my hair poppers were pretty good and other[...] left a lot to be desired. In time, with a lot of practice, I [...]elt my hair poppers [...]ere good enough to not have to h[...]ng my head in shame if a [...]lity fly fisher saw them.

For me teaching other people to construct spun-hair flies was a natural step in my personal growth as a tier. However, for the new spun-hair tiers, even distribution of hair around the hook can be a real challenge. As you saw in the last fly a true-rotary vise takes much of the mystery out of the equation. Applying the hair to the hook for a popper is not much different than it is for tying a Goddard Caddis so I'm going to take less time (and steps) to explain the process. If you don't quite remember how to spin the hair using the rotating feature of the vise then refer to the previous fly.

Deer Hair Popper

Hook:	Size 2/0 to 4, sproat wet-fly style
Thread:	Lime green, color of choice
Tag:	Thread, optional
Tail:	Lime green bucktail
Collar:	Lime green deer hair, flared using two bundles
Head/body:	Green deer hair, spun & trimmed
Legs:	Rubber leg material, optional
Eyes:	Stick-on or doll eyes, optional

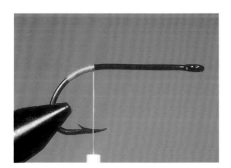

Step 1: Place the hook in the vise and apply a thread base that starts at the end of the hook shank. Wrap it down into the hook bend and back to the starting point. Trim off the waste thread end. This step anchors the thread to the hook and at the same time constructs the tag. It can also anchor a strip of monofilament to the hook to later use as a weed guard should you choose this optional step.

Step 2: Select a clump of green-dyed bucktail and remove the short fibers. I like to even the tips somewhat via hand stacking but did not use a hair stacker on the illustrated fly. Tie the hair to the hook to form a tail that is one and one-half times the length of the hook shank. Trim the waste ends. Notice I placed one loop of thread between the tail and the hook to lift/separate it from the tag.

Step 3: There are several methods for constructing the hair collar. On this fly I'm going to complete it using two bunches of deer hair flared in position. Select a clump of deer hair, remove the under fur, and even the tips in a stacker. Measure the bundle so it is equal to the length of the hook shank and trim off the excess fibers. Tie the trimmed clump of hair to the off side of the hook with a couple of tight thread wraps.

Step 4: Select a second clump of deer hair about equal in size to the first and remove the under fur. Even the tips in a hair stacker then measure and trim the clump as outlined in the previous step. Bind it to the near side of the hook then wrap the thread forward on the hook shank a couple of turns past the flared hair.

Step 5: Remember how to spin hair using the rotating feature of the vise. Let's spin two applications of hair on the shank then push the fibers back using a hair packer.

Step 6: Select two strands of white rubber leg material about four inches long and tie them on the hook using crisscross wraps to form legs that are about two-inches in length. I find leaving them stuck together makes trimming the fly later much easier. Spin one clump of hair in front of the legs then tie on a second set. Spin one more clump of hair. The legs have a tendency to tangle when rotating the vise so I hand spun these two hair applications. They help hold the legs out of the way so I'll spin the rest of the hair using the rotating feature of the vise.

Step 7: Spin enough hair to finish covering the rest of the hook shank. Whip-finish the thread and trim it from the hook.

Step 8: Rotate the vise one-half turn so the belly of the fly is exposed. Trim it flat from the hook eye to the end of the shank. I like to trim off the bottom of the collar so it is even with the fly's belly.

Step 9: Angle the scissors so the cut is the opposite of the one used on the Goddard Caddis; wide at the front and narrow at the back. In this illustration I've made a couple of cuts then pulled the legs out of the way to do several more.

Step 10: Finish trimming the head/body. I find using a small paintbrush helps keep waste fibers out of the way and also locates the errant strand that need additional trimming. Separate the legs to complete the fly. I like to add eyes to my poppers but that procedure is to please me only. I don't think the fish care one-way or another.

Crystal Muddler

When Gretchen and I retired from corporate America and moved to Montana to start a new life we spent the better part of two months finding, then closing on a home. During the couple of months down time waiting to get into our new house we decided to see how many streams we could fish in Montana and a couple of adjacent states. We traveled, camped, and fished jokingly referring to ourselves as "stream people." It was a great life while it lasted.

During our last weeks "on the road" we stayed at an RV park in Manhattan, Montana so we could be close to good fishing and still have fairly easy access to Bozeman where we could sign papers, meet with realtors, and prepare for the move into a new home. Our next-door neighbor in the RV park was Ron Marsh, a traveling construction worker. During a conversation at dinner one evening we mentioned our interest in fly-fishing and Ron immediately perked up telling us his brother Jim from nearby Billings really loved the sport as well.

Long story short we found ourselves meeting his brother on the Jefferson River several weeks later to enjoy a float trip together. He quietly asked me if I knew anything about rowing a drift boat and I assured him I was quite experienced. Jim's smile spoke volumes that only a fellow owner of a drift boat could understand; he would not be spending the whole day on the oars but would get a chance to fish as well. While driving him back from shuttling his truck to the end of the float I

asked Jim what flies he suggested for the river at that time of the year. He short response again spoke volumes, "A Muddler!"

When we got back to Gretchen and the boat I told her to rig up with a Muddler and down the river we headed. The section of river Jim was floating that day was fairly small, given to water fluctuation from agriculture pressures, and the banks were choked with over-hanging willows. In other words it was brown trout heaven!

We had not drifted very far when Gretchen hooked a nice brownie from a small cove in the willows. As the day unfolded we found a willing trout located in just about every small pocket in those willows but due to the presentation difficulty we lost a lot of flies in the process. Toward the end of the trip I was on the oars with Jim in the front of the boat. He happened to snag the willows and mumbled something about it being his last fly so I pulled hard on the oars moving the boat near the overhang and grabbed the willows to stabilize us in the current. I removed the fly and started to pass it back to him. What I saw stunned me. Jim's Muddler did not have a tail, body, or under-wing. Its complete dressing was a clump of turkey-tail fibers for the wing and a deer-hair collar/head. He had been taking fish throughout the day on par with us and we were fishing a complete Muddler dressing including all the parts he left off his.

On the way home that evening, Gretchen and I discussed Jim's simple dressing for his Muddler. I commented we would certainly have to modify our Muddler patterns if we were going to fish the Jefferson in the future because the willows along the banks loved the fly almost as much as the brown trout in the water did. During the course of our conversation we decided the pattern, or a variation of it, would have to join a series of flies on which we were working. At the time the series did not have a name but in due course we named them EZY Trout Flies. Who knows, there may be a future book on the series but for now my focus here is tying our version of Jim's Muddler using rotary tying techniques. If you'll notice, I just didn't have the heart to leave the body off the fly like Jim's pattern, but I did simplify it a bit. As these next steps unfold you will see just how easy tying a Muddler can be!

Note to Al from Gretchen: "Thanks for not sharing the story of my turn on the oars that day!"

Crystal Muddler

Hook:	Size 4 to 14, streamer style
Thread:	Brown
Body:	Copper Krystal Flash
Under wing:	Copper Krystal Flash
Wing:	Turkey tail slip, folded
Gills:	Red dubbing or yarn
Collar:	Spun deer hair
Head:	Spun & trimmed deer hair

Step 1: Place the hook in the vise and mentally divide the shank into four parts starting at the eye. Lay down a thread base that begins at the one-fourth position, travels to the end of the shank, and returns to the starting location. Select several strands of copper Krystal Flash, tie them to the shank at the one-fourth point, and store the thread in the bobbin rest. Hold the Krystal Flash in the right hand and rotate the vise to apply the first pass of material on the trip from the front to the back of the hook. I suggest coating the thread base with crazy glue to improve the fly's durability.

Step 2: Upon reaching the end of the shank continue rotating the vise while applying the Krystal Flash traveling forward on the hook to meet the tying thread at the one-fourth position. Tie the Krystal Flash off on top of the hook using three thread turns then fold the strands over and bind them to the shank to form the under wing. Trim the under wing so it is even with the end of the hook bend.

Step 3: Select a slip of turkey tail that is as wide as three hook gapes. Center the slip on a bodkin then fold it in half. Remove the bodkin from the folded feather. Make a second fold by laying the folded slip on top of the under wing, and position the feather down around the Krystal Flash. Adjust the folded feather's length so it is a bit longer than the under wing. Place a loose loop of thread around the folded slip, hold the feather/thread/hook between the thumb/forefinger, and tighten the thread to anchor the wing in position. Place a couple more thread wraps then trim off the waste part of the slip. Use a pair of scissors to shape (trim) the end of the wings.

Step 4: Place a small amount of red dubbing on the thread and cover the trimmed ends forming the gills. Leave the thread hanging directly to the front of the gills.

Step 5: Select a clump of deer hair and clean out the under fur. Align the hair tips in a stacker, remove them, and trim the butts to length. I like this clump of hair to be about three-fourths the length of the hook shank but I think a Muddler collar length is a personal thing so adjust yours accordingly. Set the trimmed clump straight down on the hook and hold it in place with three snug (but not tight) thread wraps. Hold the bobbin tight in the right hand and rotate the vise with the left to spin the collar. Wrap the thread one turn in front of the spun hair and leave it there for the next step.

Step 6: Select another clump of deer hair, clean out the under fur, and do not stack it. Tie the clump to the hook using three snug (but not tight) thread wraps by the butt ends and trim off the tips. Again, hold the bobbin tight in the right hand and use the left hand to rotate the vise thus spinning the hair.

Step 7: Select a third clump of hair and remove the under fur. Tie it to the hook with three thread wraps (snug but not tight) with the TIPS pointing forward. Do not trim them off. Rotate the vise to spin this last application of hair. You'll note the long tips in front really make it easier to keep them out of the way while constructing a whip-finish. After tying off the thread, trim it from the hook.

Step 8: Rotate the vise so the belly of the fly is facing up and trim the head flat even with the body. I like my collar trimmed flat on the bottom so the gills show through but like a lot of things in fly tying it is a personal preference. Now rotate the vise slowly while making a series of clips with the scissors. In no time at all you will have a perfectly trimmed head if you use the rotating feature of the vise to turn the fly while keeping the scissors in one position. If you own a curved pair of scissors this is a great place to give them a try.

Chapter 9: Fisker Design

Foam Stone

Like a lot of western trout anglers I've spent more than a little time chasing that Holy Grail of fly-fishing experience, the salmonfly hatch! I can't tell you the number of times over the years I heard the dreaded words from fellow fly-fishers, "You should have been here yesterday!" At that time I was a manager in corporate America and the demands of my job never did coincide with nature. I missed the major part of every hatch I pursued for the better part of fifteen years. I had the desire and the perfect fly but that didn't make a bit of difference if the timing was off! If you didn't catch the words in the last sentence "perfect fly" then I'll bring it to your attention. How did I know I had the perfect fly? The friends I shared this pattern with told me it was a great fly that caught lots of trout for them. I just never proved it to myself.

Then came the day when Gretchen and I retired and moved to Montana to start the rest of our lives as part of the fly-fishing industry. For the next five years I never missed the salmonfly hatch. Yes, the Foam Stone was a great pattern; it just took me the better part of fifteen years to prove it to myself. During those five years I also learned a lot about the salmonfly hatch. I learned the fishing was usually better just before or for several weeks after the actual hatch. During the hatch the fish were so full of the bugs they wouldn't move much more than a couple of inches to capture a natural insect let alone an imitation. Their attitude really changed as the days unfolded after the hatch while the fish still had short-term memory of the large insects.

Gretchen and I use its general design for almost all of our stonefly patterns. All we have to do is change the color and size of the pattern for it to represent a wide range of insects including several larger mayflies. Of course, if you use the body design on a mayfly you have to change the wing style but that is really quite easy to do.

Not only am I sharing a great pattern with all of you, I'm also going to explain a tip about bullet heads—correcting a mistake where there is not enough hair on the hook to produce a properly proportioned head. First though we need to put a needle in the vise to construct the foam extended body.

Foam Stone

Hook:	Size 8, standard dry fly
Thread:	Hot orange
Tail:	Turkey biots
Rib:	Thread tied in bands
Body:	Black closed-cell foam
Wings:	Elk hair
Collar:	Black dyed deer hair
Bullet head:	Black dyed deer hair
Legs:	Silicone or rubber leg material

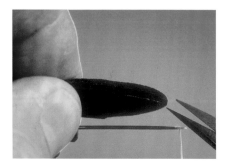

Step 1: Place a needle in the vise jaws or in a tube-fly tool with the point facing to the right. I like to use a fairly blunt-pointed needle for obvious reasons. Place three turns of thread on the needle very near the point. Cut a strip of foam about four inches long that is a wide as the gape of the hook. Fold the foam strip in half and trim the folded part to a blunt point.

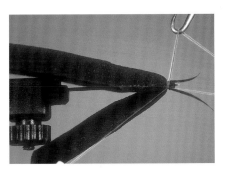

Step 2: Sandwich the folded strip around the needle and push the point through the foam. Bind the foam to the end of the needle with several thread wraps. Select two black (or color of choice) biots, tie one on either side of the needle/foam, and trim the waste ends. Whip-finish, trim the thread from the needle, and apply a coating of Aqua Head. I mentioned "color of choice" regarding the biots in the tail because we have had great luck with flies made using hot colors like orange, pink, or chartreuse. You may want to try some of those colors as well.

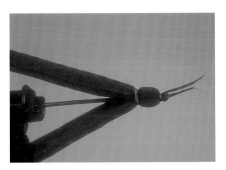

Step 3: Move back on the needle about one-fourth inch and wrap another band of hot orange thread. Whip-finish it, trim the thread from the needle, and apply a coating of Aqua Head. Slip the tail section off the needle but leave the second segment positioned near the point.

Step 4: Construct two more bands of orange thread slipping one off each time another is completed. Whip-finish and glue each as directed in the previous steps. Set this extended body aside and construct as many more as you will need to fill your fly box.

Step 5: Take the needle out of the vise and replace it with a size-eight hook. Place four thread wraps tight against the hook eye then apply a single half hitch to keep the thread from slipping. Select a clump of black deer hair, clean out the under fur, and align the tips in a hair stacker. Remove the hair from the stacker and trim the clump so it is as long as the complete hook. Hold the hair at the hook eye with the tips forward and place three turns of thread (snug but not tight) around the butt ends. Hold the bobbin firm in the right hand and rotate the vise with the left. As the thread gets shorter increasing tension, the clump of hair will spin around the hook. After spinning the hair I find I did not apply enough material to form the bullet head, I only have half as much hair as I really needed. To correct this problem wrap the thread back away from the spun hair about three turns and leave the bobbin there for the next step.

Step 6: Select, clean, and stack a second clump of black hair. Trim it to length and spin it behind the first clump of hair. The reason I moved back on the hook shank was to avoid snagging the hair fibers from the second clump with those in the first. Now that the second clump of hair is distributed around the hook I'll use my hair packer (or fingers) to press it tight against the first. You'll never know about the mistake when viewing the completed fly.

Chapter 9: Fisker Design

Step 7: Retrieve one of the extended bodies constructed in the first several steps and tie it to the center of the hook. Trim off the waste ends. Some of my friends like to "thread" the foam body on the hook before binding it in place but I've never found a need to do so.

Step 8: Select a clump of elk hair, remove the under fur, and even the tips in a stacker. Remove the clump of hair from the stacker and tie it to the hook to form a Trude style wing that is as long as the extended body. Trim the waste ends of hair.

Step 9: Fold the bullet-head hair over using a tool or fingers to dress the fibers back. Bind the head in place then remove the tool. The tube on the Backcast bullet-head tool is clear allowing me to make certain the hair fibers are evenly placed.

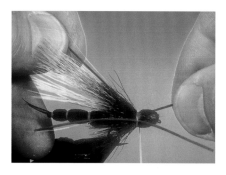

Step 10: Select two rubber leg segments that are equal in length and tie them both to the near side of the fly. Move the top leg to the off side of the hook then apply a whip-finish. Trim the thread from the hook and apply a coating of Aqua Flex to complete the fly. Note: When I tied the two legs on the near side of the hook then moved one to the off side there was no doubt whether they were aligned with each other. This method is a lot easier than trying to get them even while tying the legs on the hook one at a time.

Waker Wulff

Gretchen and I assembled this pattern on a request from a commercial fly customer who gave us a straightforward directive, "I don't care what it is, just tie me a steelhead dry fly that will float like crazy and really skip across the water's surface."

This fly didn't just happen; it evolved over the next couple of years. We tried heavily hackling it, putting a moose hair skipping beard on it, and a short, stiff plastic sliding spoon on it. Nothing seemed to work like the

customer really wanted. Finally one day we decided to go back to the days I tied small hair, hackle dry flies. Those flies had floated great we just needed to find out if hair hackle would also make them skip over the water's surface. They did! The customer was happy and of course, we were as well!

You might think the story would end there and it certainly could have. Gretchen and I tie a lot of custom flies and don't always fish with them. There is just not the time to fish with everything we tie on a commercial basis. However, the Waker Wulff did find its way into one of my fly boxes I keep in the drift boat but remained unused for a couple of years. One fall afternoon we were drifting the Yellowstone River and even though the fishing was great the catching was real slow. Out of desperation I tied it on my tippet, punched a cast to the bank, let it set for a moment, and then gave it two hard strips. The water exploded as a heavy brown trout grabbed it and headed to the middle of the river. A sleepy afternoon quickly changed into an adrenaline-charged super day.

Does this fly always work this well? No, it does not but it has saved more than one trout-fishing day for us. It may do the same for you as well. We also consider it an important addition to our steelhead fly box. There is nothing like catching a steelhead on a dry fly as is skitters across the water's surface. Gretchen and I have not yet tried it on chinook salmon but that experiment will be behind us by the time you read these words.

Waker Wulff

Hook:	Size 2 to 10, steelhead
Thread:	Fire orange single-strand floss, color of choice
Tail:	Moose body hair
Wing:	Calf tail
Hackle:	Deer hair
Head:	Thread

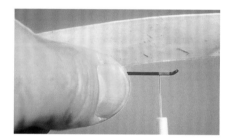

Step 1: Place the hook in the vise and lay down a thread base that starts at the eye and stops at the end of the looped-eye platform. Clip a three-inch section of masking tape from a roll and stick it to your thumb several times so most of the tackiness is removed but not all of it. Set the tape strip aside for a moment.

Step 2: Select a clump of deer hair, clean out the under fur, and even the tips in a stacker. Trim the butt ends of the clump so the fiber's length is equal to the hook shank. Tie the clump on the hook with the tips facing forward at the start of the looped-eye platform with three turns of thread (remember, snug but not tight). Hold the bobbin tight in the right hand and rotate the vise with the left to spin the hair around the hook. Recover the strip of masking tape prepared in the previous step and place it over the top of the spun hair. The purpose of the tape is to keep the calf tail in the next step separated from the deer hair.

Step 3: Select a clump of calf-tail fibers, remove the under fur/short fibers, and even the tips in a stacker. Tie the calf tail, tips forward, to the hook as a wing clump that is a bit shorter than the deer hair in the previous step. Trim off the waste ends of calf tail. With the thread positioned behind the calf tail, divide the material into two wing posts. Wrap a couple of thread turns around each and anchor them in place so they are tilted slightly forward. Now you can remove the strip of masking tape.

Step 4: The trimmed calf-tail fibers remaining from the wings make it very difficult to spin the next clump of hair. Therefore, I'm going to tie it to the hook similar to the method I used on the Deer Hair Popper earlier in this chapter only I'll point the tips forward instead of back. Select, clean, and stack a clump of deer hair. Tie it to the shank (tips forward) on the under side of the hook with several tight thread wraps, make sure their length is equal to the hair placed in Step 2. Trim the waste ends then spread the flared hair so it is flared across the bottom half of the hook. Repeat the process on the top of the hook to finish forming the part of the hackle behind the wings.

Step 5: Select a clump of moose hair, clean out the under fur, and even the tips in a stacker. Measure the stacked hair so it is long enough to form a tail equal to the length of the hook shank plus the shank itself then trim off the rest off at the butt end. Set the trimmed ends tight against the back of the second clump of deer hair hackle. Wrap over the hair to the end of the shank and back to the starting point forming the body.

Step 6: Work the thread through the back hackle, then around the wings, and through the front hackle. Wrap a thread dam tight against the front hackle to force it to stand up. Whip-finish the thread, trim it from the hook, and apply a coating of Aqua Head to finish the fly.

Green Sweeper

This fly fell from my vise while Gretchen and I were working on the *Fly Pattern Encyclopedia*. I was tying a Gray Macintosh for the Steelhead, Salmon, and Rangeley Flies section of the book and Gretchen was working on an order of Stimulators where the customer had requested green dubbing on the head. After finishing the Macintosh I placed another salmon hook in the vise and tied on the tinsel portion of a tag. I tried to toss the gray squirrel tail back in its storage box and missed. After picking it up and placing it in the container I saw a fox squirrel tail had mistakenly found its way into the box for the gray. I grabbed the tail with good intentions of returning it to its home but got distracted by Gretchen. It ended up on the tying table next to the elk hair, grizzly hackle, and green dubbing she was using on her Stimulator order.

One thing led to another and those darned materials just jumped off the table and attached themselves to the hook in my vise while I was out of the room getting a cup of coffee. When I returned to the vise we discussed including this unusual, self-constructed fly in the book, decided it was a good idea, and set the pattern aside until we could assign a name. After work that day I cleaned up the tying room before retiring for the night.

The next morning I returned to my work station and the fly was no where to be found. I looked high and low. It had vanished! I mentioned to Gretchen the name we

had selected for it (The Mistake) seemed very appropriate; it really was the result of a whole series of mistakes and now it was missing.

I found the fly later the next day when taking out the weekly trash. When I emptied my waste bag there it was sitting on top of the remnants of the last several days' work. I must have swept into my trash bag while cleaning up the previous evening. The fly immediately got a name change from The Mistake to the Green Sweeper.

You might think the story would end there; not so! I never got to fish steelhead with the fly for a couple of years until Gretchen and I moved home to Idaho. On my first trip to fish the Salmon River I knew I had to give the ole Sweeper a test drive. I ran it through several likely looking runs but the steelhead there-in just ignored my offering. After several unsuccessful presentations I finally got a solid hook-up. When I landed the fish it was not a steelhead; instead I had a bull trout on the end of my line. I clipped the Sweeper from my line and retired it on the spot. It started from a series of mistakes and continued that behavior pattern all the way to the water. Maybe a brave soul reading these pages will feel lucky enough to give the Sweeper a try—who knows, they might even be successful. With me, it's had a last chance—for fishing that is! It does hold a good rotary lesson or two so I'll give it one more chance to redeem itself.

Green Sweeper

Hook:	Size 2 to 10, steelhead
Thread:	Fire orange
Tag:	Fine silver tinsel & thread
Wing:	Fox squirrel under elk hair
Head/body:	Green Seal-Ex, thread
Hackle:	Grizzly, palmered

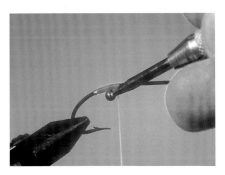

Step 1: Place the hook in the vise and apply four thread wraps to the shank directly above the point. Tie the fine tinsel to the underside of the hook then bind it down into the bend stopping at a location above the throat of the barb. Wind a five-turn tinsel application, tie it off (again on the underside), and bind the loose end to the bottom of the hook while wrapping back to the starting point. Trim the waste ends of tinsel then apply another layer of thread over the first by wrapping down to meet the tinsel application and back to the starting point. I like to smooth the thread wraps with a burnishing tool to give the tag a glossy appearance.

Step 2: Wrap the thread forward to the center of the hook and leave it there for a moment. Select a clump of fox squirrel tail, clean out the under fur, and even the tips in a hair stacker. Tie them to the back half of the hook so they form a wing as long as the shank then trim the waste ends at a fairly severe angle to provide part of the hackle platform needed in a future step. Laying the scissors flat along the shank produces the angle I need.

Step 3: Wind the thread forward about half way to the hook eye thus binding the trimmed squirrel fibers to the shank. Select, clean, and stack a clump of elk hair. Bind it to the hook forming an over wing equal in length to the squirrel fibers already in place. Again, trim the waste ends using the same scissor placement as demonstrated in the previous step. Wrap over the trimmed ends leaving the thread hanging near the back of the hook.

Step 4: Select a grizzly saddle feather gauged for a hook two sizes smaller than the one in the vise. In my illustration I'm tying the fly on a size-two hook and using a number-six feather. Remove the fuzzy material at the base of the stem and tie it to the hook while advancing the thread forward to meet the eye. Temporarily store the feather in the material keeper. Remove a clump of green Seal-Ex from its package and tease out a several-inch strand of loose dubbing.

Chapter 9: Fisker Design

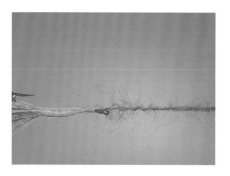

Step 5: Anchor the tip of the teased out dubbing to the hook with a turn or two of thread. Hold the thread and dubbing in front of the vise and rotate it to form a dubbing rope.

Step 6: Bring the dubbing rope perpendicular to the hook and continue rotating the vise to apply it starting at the front and ending back at the hackle. Pull the excess dubbing from the thread.

Step 7: Remove the hackle from the material keeper and bring it (don't forget the thread) perpendicular with the hook. Rotate the vise to advance the feather/thread combination forward to the hook eye. Did you remember to use the traveling bobbin rest or the drop tie off? If you have forgotten, those techniques were reviewed in Chapter Four.

Step 8: Trim off the feather, build a thread head, apply a whip-finish, and clip the thread from the hook. I like to complete the fly with a coat of Aqua Flex or Aqua Tuff; either one produces a smooth, glossy head.

10

Griffin Enterprises, Inc.

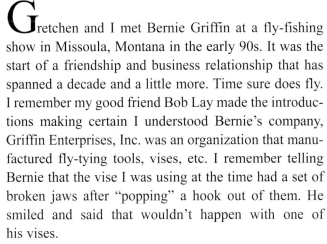

Gretchen and I met Bernie Griffin at a fly-fishing show in Missoula, Montana in the early 90s. It was the start of a friendship and business relationship that has spanned a decade and a little more. Time sure does fly. I remember my good friend Bob Lay made the introductions making certain I understood Bernie's company, Griffin Enterprises, Inc. was an organization that manufactured fly-tying tools, vises, etc. I remember telling Bernie that the vise I was using at the time had a set of broken jaws after "popping" a hook out of them. He smiled and said that wouldn't happen with one of his vises.

The show ended, we said our goodbyes, and drove home to Wenatchee, Washington where I was employed as a District Manager for a large utility company. Darned if a package didn't show up in the mail the next week with two Griffin's Patriot vises inside—a gift from Bernie. What a surprise! To say we were delighted was an understatement. It only took us a few minutes to set up the new toys and start putting them through their paces. We were especially pleased with the hook-holding ability and how easy it was to close the cam-operated jaws. The old vises have enjoyed a forced retirement ever since. Note from Gretchen: When Al's not looking, I still use mine for certain flies!

A couple weeks later Bernie called to see if the vises had arrived safely. We assured him they had and told him a package was in the mail to him. The conversation rambled over a number of subjects when we got around to telling him we would soon join him in Montana. Expanding on the subject, I advised him we had decided to move to Bozeman to start a second career guiding and tying flies. He thought that sounded like a good idea and ended his phone call telling us to stay in touch.

Shortly thereafter (May 15, 1993 to be exact) we retired and headed to Montana. We spent the whole summer fishing as many different waters as possible. It was a great time but as summer's last days gave way to fall's vivid colors we finally settled on a house and moved in. It was just one week before the Federation of Fly Fishers Conclave in Livingston. It was a wild time getting our belongings unpacked before leaving for the Conclave. We did manage to get most everything stored somewhere before guests attending the Conclave started arriving at our new home.

At the show we again bumped into Bernie where we shared our summer's experiences with him. I made sure he knew the two vises didn't end up in a storage box, they traveled right along with us in a tying kit we assembled before leaving Wenatchee. He asked if I could recommend any changes. I suggested fine-pointed jaws and a couple weeks later a prototype set arrived in the mail. I still use them today over ten years later.

Bernie started his business, Griffin Enterprises, Inc., quite by accident. In the early 70s his regular day job was in the lumber industry. During slack times he would tie flies for the Streamside Angler in Missoula, Montana not far from his home in Bonner. It didn't take very many orders of flies for Bernie to look for something different to do rather than spending hours at the vise; that just wasn't for him. Streamside Angler owners Rich Andersen and Frank Johnson encouraged him to make tying tools; he started with a bobbin. Not long after he began manufacturing a two-piece hair evener (one of the first in the industry as he remembers).

More tools came from Bernie's machine shop as the 70s melted into the 80s. Near the end of the 80s he developed his first vise, the 2A following the next year with the 1A. By the time I met him in the early 90s he had several vises on the market including the Patriot I mentioned a couple of paragraphs ago. The cam jaws' closing mechanism was one of the first on the market. Bernie told me he got the idea for the cam style while "messing around" with a set of regular jaws and a screwdriver. When he twisted the screwdriver one way the jaws closed, the other way opened them. Of course the light bulb went on from there and now we "know the rest of the story" as Paul Harvey would say. Today the Griffin product line consists of nine different bobbin styles, nine unique vises, and over thirty accessory tools. Somewhere along the line Bernie quit his day job and devoted all of his time to manufacturing fly-tying tools. I'm glad he did; all of his products are good quality, manufactured in Montana, very reasonably priced, and I'm proud to be one of his distributors. When Gretchen and I decided to get into the fly-fishing/tying business, Bernie was one of the people who influenced us to select the direction we went. He has been a major influence in our fly-tying lives for a number of years; we are pleased to call him mentor/friend.

In this chapter I'm going to tie flies on two of Bernie's vises. I've used/sold the Odyssey Cam for several years and it originally is the vise I selected to feature here. When I spoke with Bernie a few weeks ago about this book he told me to keep an eye on the mail. Darned if another package didn't show up with the Montana Mongoose (vise) in it a few days later. I only tied a few flies on it and decided that awesome vise had to be part of the book. Wait till you see how one of its adjustment features makes weaving a fly body a real "piece of cake."

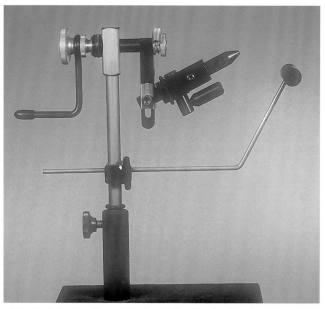

I had originally planned to tie all the flies in this chapter on the Odyssey Cam but the arrival of the Montana Mongoose changed my mind.

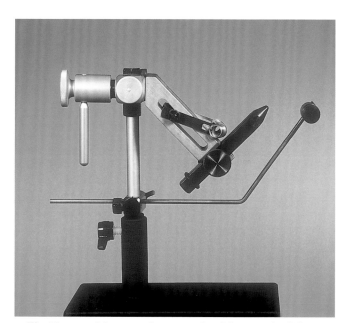

The Montana Mongoose has a couple of features the Odyssey Cam does not, therefore I felt it was important to feature it in this chapter as well.

Hot Spot Bomber

This pattern is the result of a mistake I made on an order of flies I was tying for a customer planning a steelhead trip to Canada. Among other things, the customer had asked for a dozen Bombers tied with red and orange thread—six of each color. I tied the six using orange thread then switched to red to finish the dozen. On the last fly I broke the thread spinning the last clump of hair, the one at the end of the hook shank (that may sound confusing but you'll see why the last bundle of hair was directly adjacent to the tail in a few minutes). I reattached the broken thread, spun the last clump of

hair, and finished the fly like I normally would. I started to put it in the box of flies I was sending to the customer and thought better of it. What if the fly fell apart? I certainly didn't want that so instead I put the fly in my personal box and tied another Bomber for my customer. I then sent the flies to him knowing I had done my best to provide good, durable patterns.

The fly remained in my box for more than a year until one day I was fishing for steelhead on the Clearwater River in central Idaho. I was taking a pretty bad whipping using my standard wet-style flies. The

Clearwater is not known for producing a lot of steelhead on dry flies but I thought, "What the heck, I'm not catching anything now!" About the third or fourth fly I tried was this "broken thread" Bomber. I only made a half-a-dozen casts when I saw a small piece of hair separate from the fly and head down stream. I stripped the fly in to see what was happening and discovered my repair job on the Bomber more than a year earlier didn't last very long. The last clump of hair was gone and exposed under it was the red thread holding the tail in place.

I figured what the heck, I would give a try anyway. I guarantee you, I wasn't having that great of a day and the sunlight wasn't far from giving way to twilight. On my first cast over a likely holding-lie a fish came up and took a swipe at the fly. I missed it not knowing whether it was my fault (asleep at the wheel after a long, boring day) or the steelhead refused it at the last minute. I figured I'd rest the fish for a few minutes and then give it another chance. After a short break I ran the fly over it again and this time I didn't miss it. What had been a boring day suddenly exploded into an adrenaline-charged super outing.

Now I'd like to tell you a really good fish story about all the steelhead I caught on that fly afterward but it just wouldn't be true. What really happened was I moved downstream to another likely looking spot and hung the fly in a willow that snuck into my back cast when I was looking the other way. I'm the kind of guy that never goes after tangled flies. I just break them off and tie on another BUT I knew that fly was the only Bomber I had with red hot spot on it.

I set my rod aside and reviewed my situation. The fly was higher than I could reach and the willow seemed too small to climb but you never know until you've tried. I should have listened to that "little warning voice" in the back of my head because I went after that fly! The willow broke dropping me down the bank landing me on my fly rod. It broke with a sickening "crack." The jagged end of the broken willow practically tore one leg off my waders and I got pretty skinned up in the process. Looking back on it now it sounds kind of funny but at the time I wasn't doing much laughing. I picked up the pieces of my outfit and started the 150-mile drive home. It turned out to be one long drive as the damaged parts of my body were soon telling me in no uncertain terms that I had not treated them very well!

That little episode kept me close to home for several weeks. On the positive side, I had plenty of time to tie flies and I whipped up a bunch of Hot Spot Bombers. I can't tell you it was a discovery that made all future fishing trips a roaring success but that ole Bomber did catch a lot of fish for me in the years following. In fact, if you look through my personal fly boxes you'll see a lot of flies with hot spots or tags on them. Do hot spot flies work better than others? I really can't say but I sure catch a lot of fish with them. Years later when Gary LaFontaine and I talked about his theory on "strike zones" his words helped me verbalize what had been stuck in my mind over the years looking for a way out. The hot spot seems to provide the fish an area on which to focus, or as Gary called it, a strike zone.

I'm tying this pattern using the Odyssey Cam vise. The rotating feature really helps in the pattern's construction. I think you will notice right off I don't tie it like a traditional Bomber. Maybe this construction technique will give some of you a few ideas.

Hot Spot Bomber

Hook:	Size 2 to 10, salmon fly
Thread:	Red, or hot color of choice
Tail:	Calf-tail hair
Body:	Spun & trimmed deer hair
Wing:	Calf tail, tied as a post
Hackle:	Brown saddle
Hot spots:	Thread at each end of the fly

Chapter 10: Griffin Enterprises, Inc.

Step 1: Place the hook in the vise and attach the tying thread to the shank slightly forward of point. Wrap a short thread base from that position down slightly into the bend and back to the starting location. Select a clump of calf-tail hair, clean out the short fibers, and even the tips in a stacker. Tie them to the hook to form a tail as long as the hook shank. Cut any waste ends, whip-finish the thread, and trim it from the hook.

Step 2: Reattach the thread directly behind the eye and lay down a short base that covers the looped-back platform. Select, clean, and stack a clump of calf-tail hair. Tie it to the hook to form a single wing post (tips forward) that is as long as the shank. Trim off the waste ends then cover them with several thread turns. Build a small thread dam in front of the wing post to force it to stand up part of the way. I like an angle of about forty-five degrees, more or less. Leave the thread hanging behind the wings.

Step 3: The thread, covered area behind the wings can be a problem to spin hair over so instead I'm going to flare it in two steps. Select a clump of deer hair and remove the under fur. Tie it to the off side of the hook with three snug but not tight thread wraps then trim off the hair tips. When I apply pressure to the thread the hair will flare and slip to the bottom of the shank covering that part of the hook.

Step 4: Select a second clump of deer hair and remove the under fur. Tie it to the top of the hook with three snug wraps then trim off the tips. Tighten the thread turns to flare the hair in place covering the top of the hook. Wrap the thread back through the hair and leave it hanging directly behind the two-clump hair application. Use fingers or a packing tool to push the hair fibers forward.

Step 5: Use a bodkin to separate the flared deer hair from the calf tail wing post. Select a clump of deer hair and remove the under fur. Tie it to the top of the hook with three snug (but not tight) thread turns then clip off the hair tips. Hold the thread/bobbin firmly in the right hand and use the left to rotate the vise. The hair will spin evenly around the hook after rotating the vise a couple of turns. Use fingers or a packing tool to push this clump of hair forward against the fibers from Step 4. Wrap the thread back through the hair so it is on bare hook behind the spun hair. Repeat the complete process again leaving the thread hanging behind the spun hair.

Step 6: Use the same procedure as outlined in Step 5 to apply as many clumps of hair as needed to cover the rest of the hook shank. In the illustrated fly it took three more bundles of hair but the hook size and shank length determines the amount required.

Step 7: Trim the body to shape. I like to start by trimming the bottom (as illustrated) as close to the hook shank as possible. If you rotate the vise while holding the scissors stationary it is quite easy to trim a symmetrically shaped body. Also, if you trim with the scissors on top, the thread is always hanging down out of harm's way.

Step 8: Select a brown saddle hackle and prepare it by stripping the fuzzy fibers from the base of the stem. Tie it to the hook at the back of the body. I find it quite easy to hide the excess feather stem in trimmed body. When I wrap the feather over the hidden stem it is further anchored by that process as well. Hold the feather and thread between the right thumb and forefinger. Rotate the vise with the left hand to palmer the hackle/thread through the body. Tie off the feather and trim away the excess. Apply a whip-finish then trim the thread from the hook. I like to complete the fly with a coat of Aqua Tuff on the head and the hot spot. Author's Note: You might be wondering why I spun the hair from the front of the hook to the back. It's really quite simple. It's one way I have found to keep from stabbing my fingers on the hook point when packing a newly spun bundle of hair against the previous clump.

Mottled Carrie

Last weekend Gretchen and I spent a couple of days on a local bluegill pond. We had a great time, caught lots of fish, and recharged our batteries; something we both needed. I especially had a good time because it is always great to watch Gretchen catch fish; her giggle just brightens my day for some reason. Maybe that's why I'm married to her; there is a lot about her that brightens my day.

On most trips she outfishes me but Saturday morning was a different story. For once I caught more fish than she did. It wasn't long before she pulled her pontoon boat beside mine on the pretext of visiting with our dog Dubbin. Let me digress for a moment. For those of you who don't know Dubbin, he is our 100-pound chocolate lab "fishing dog." He rides on a specially built platform on the back of my pontoon boat and loves fishing almost as much as we do.

Anyway, back to my story. After petting Dubbing for a couple of minutes she finally asked me what fly I'm using. I told her a Carrie Special with a mottled body on a full-sink "slim line." I had an extra full-sink line so I offered my rod to her. Our outfits were identical so it made no difference to me which rod I used. She accepted my offer, kicked her boat about thirty feet from mine, made a cast, and was immediately into a

fish. The sound of her giggle drifted across the water as I rigged her rod with a new line and fly.

As I tied on another Mottled Carrie I though back to the time when I first learned of this pattern from John Newbury from Chewelah, Washington. He had invited me to join him on a private lake in northeast Washington where the fish were big, hot, and aggressive. We dragged our equipment and float tubes to the water's edge (you see this was the days before individual pontoon boats). John advised me it would be best to start with a full-sink line and whatever pattern I thought would be good. I noted he tied on a dark Carrie Special so I followed suit with one of my own; I think it was olive if I remember right.

He wasn't in the water more than a few minutes when he hooked a nice rainbow. I was still on the bank getting my equipment changed over from a standard stream fishing setup to a full-sink, down-and-dirty rig. When I finally slipped my float tube over my head and backed into the water John had caught and released three fish. I was expecting great fishing but it didn't happen, at least not for me. I studied what he was doing, his countdown, the time frame, the part of the lake, and especially the retrieve. As close as I could, I mimicked everything he did. An hour later I had caught two fish and John must have released a dozen or more. It was time to find out what I should be doing different. I kicked over to him and asked what I could change. We compared rigs and found they were basically the same. When I looked at his fly the body had a variegated glint while lying in his hand and mine did not. I asked him about the difference. He had woven strands of tinsel into the body to form lateral lines on either side. That seemed to be the only difference. He gave me several of his flies and my luck changed immediately. No, I didn't do better than John but I had a pretty awesome

day after switching to the Carrie Special with the mottled body.

Over the years the Mottled Carrie has served me well in a variety of stillwater environments. Like a lot of my flies, I've added a bright colored tag to it and in most situations it seems to produce better for me than a fly without a hot spot. In the next several paragraphs I'll explain how to use a bundle of Krystal Flash to make the tag and the lateral line. The Odyssey Cam does a great job of allowing me to access the two sides of the hook to make the weaving process much easier.

Mottled Carrie

Hook:	Size 4 to 12, wet fly
Thread:	Black
Tag:	Krystal Flash, color of choice
Body:	Black Brazilian Velour
Lateral lines:	Krystal Flash from the tag
Hackle:	Pheasant rump feather
Head:	Thread or optional bead

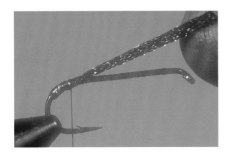

Step 1: Place the hook in the vise and wrap a thread base from slightly behind the hook eye to the end of the shank. Select a clump of Krystal Flash and tie it to the under side of the hook traveling down into the bend. Hold the Krystal Flash and thread in the right hand and use the left to rotate the vise while applying the tag. Tie the Krystal Flash off on TOP of the hook with several thread wraps.

Step 2: Divide the bundle of Krystal Flash into two units. Pull one unit back and to the near side of the hook then bind it there with a couple of thread wraps. Pull the other unit back and to the far side of the hook then bind it there with several thread wraps. Anchor each bundle in the material keeper making certain they remain separated. Wrap the thread forward to the front of the hook. Select a several inch segment of black Brazilian Velour and tie it to the top of the hook shank, from the front to the back then return again to the starting point. Store the thread in the bobbin rest.

Step 3: Grasp the Velour with the right hand and rotate the vise twice thus applying two turns of the body. Don't let go of the Velour. Retrieve the near side bundle of Krystal Flash from the material keeper and lay it over the two Velour turns. Anchor that bundle with ONE-HALF turn of Velour then pull it back into the material keeper. Retrieve the off side bundle of Krystal Flash and pull it over the other side of the two turns of Velour then anchor it with the OTHER Half turn of Velour. Pull that bundle back into the material keeper. I've just completed one mottled weave on each side of the hook. In this case the weave is "over two, under one." Construct several more weaves following the same weave pattern—over two, under one.

Step 4: The last weave is two turns of Velour anchored by a couple of turns of thread then trim off the excess material. Pull the off side Krystal Flash bundle forward, tie it off, and clip the waste ends. Repeat the same process with the near side bundle of Krystal Flash. Cover wrap over the trimmed Krystal Flash ends.

Step 5: Select a pheasant rump feather and prepare it by stripping the fuzzy material from the base of the stem. Tie it to the hook by the stem and trim any excess material. Notice I tied the stem down with several thread turns then folded it over and anchored it again to keep it from pulling out.

Step 6: Wrap a two-turn collar, tie it off, and trim the waste part of the feather. Build a thread head, whip-finish, and trim it from the hook. Complete the fly with a coating of Aqua Head. Let me share a couple of ideas on the mottled body. I like the two-over-one-under weave for cloudy days because the fly is slightly brighter. On really bright days I prefer the over-one-under-two weave because the fly is not quite as bright.

Bitch Creek Nymph

For me, this pattern means a lot more than "a fly to catch fish." It represents transition in my life on a couple of different fronts. The first transition was in my personal life taking me from a hectic military environment back to a less stressful, civilian life.

In the mid 60s I went to work for Pacific Telephone and Telegraph Company in Merced, California as an Installer/Repairman. About a year after starting employment with that company I was drafted into the US Army. I spent the next two years doing what many young men in my generation did, stateside training then a tour in Vietnam. In early 1969 I returned to my job at PT&T. I've thanked my lucky stars on more than one occasion that job was waiting for me upon my return. A few weeks after going back to work my supervisor asked me if I wanted to perform another "tour of duty," namely as a combination technician in Yosemite National Park. The job was temporary for the summer months. It sure sounded good to me and in fact it turned out to be great duty for me on both a professional basis, as well as personal. In that environment I was constantly pushed to learn new skills because often I was the only technician within several hundred miles of a customer's

need. Over the years skills I learned during that time in my life often gave me an edge during my climb up the corporate ladder.

During this same timeframe I learned new skills in my personal/fishing life. Up to this time all my fly-fishing had focused on warmwater species. I had never fished for trout in any type environment and suddenly I land in the middle of California's best. I had to go through another transition from popping bugs to dry flies, nymphs/wets, and streamers. I wasn't quite sure how to learn about trout fishing but ole PT&T had always provided for me and this situation was no different. One of the technicians I worked with (over the telephone) from the toll test center in Sacramento was an avid fly-fisher. He gave me a lot of advice and sample flies to duplicate at my own vise.

The Bitch Creek Nymph was one of those patterns. I caught my first trout on it out of the Merced River just outside the Park near El Portal, California. Wow! What a great experience! It was about fourteen inches long however when I saw it jump the first time I though it was closer to twenty. Over the years I've learned that all jumping fish tend to look bigger that they really are.

Maybe that's why the "one that got away" was always a BIG FISH. Anyway, my temporary assignment in Yosemite Park ended up lasting four years until a promotion pulled me back to Merced. During those years I fished almost all evenings after work and many weekends as well. I will always remember my time in Yosemite Park with fond memories. There I became a well-rounded technician, a heck of a good coldwater fly-fisher, and happily readjusted to civilian life.

I also learned a lot about fly-tying during those four years as I transitioned from warmwater popping bugs to trout flies. I didn't know how to weave and had to take apart my sample Bitch Creek to figure out how it went together. I assure you the weaving technique I learned from disassembling the fly looked a bunch different than the method I'll present here today. I struggled with weaving (and a lot of other tying techniques) until I attended my first Federation of Fly Fisher's Conclave in the late 70s. I learned more about tying in a couple of days at that show than I had learned on my own during the previous ten years. Fly tiers today don't know how lucky they are to have organizations like the Federation or the Internet and the wealth of knowledge each brings to the table.

I like to weave (either the parallel or over-hand) with the eye of the hook facing away from me. On the other hand Gretchen would rather complete the same weave with the hook eye facing her. Whichever way you find easier getting the hook in that position with the Mongoose is quite easy, as you will see on the next couple flies.

Bitch Creek Nymph

Hook:	Size 4 to 14, nymph
Thread:	Black
Tail:	White rubber leg material
Body:	Brazilian Velour, black & orange
Hackle:	Brown
Antenna:	White rubber leg material

Step 1: Place the hook in the vise and apply a thread base that covers the complete hook shank starting and stopping at the eye. Select a several-inch segment of white rubber leg material. The strands tend to stick together; I suggest leaving them that way for now. Tie them to the hook so they extend both front and back to later form the antenna and the tail. Trim them to length but do not break them apart. Leave the thread hanging near the front of the hook. Notice I'm using one of the Griffin's ceramic bobbins on this fly.

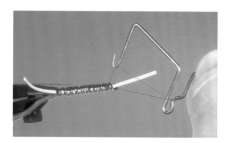

Step 2: Select a several-inch segment of black Brazilian Velour and another of orange. Tie the orange to the near side of the hook and the black to the off side of the shank. Place both temporarily in the materials keeper. Wrap the thread forward, whip-finish, and trim it temporarily from the hook. Set the bobbin aside for a moment.

Step 3: Notice I rotated the vise a partial turn in Step 2 so you can see the top of the hook. This is also the position many fly tiers select for weaving their flies. I prefer to tilt the complete vise head up from this position so the hook eye faces away from me while pointing up at a slight angle to the right. The Mongoose vise is easy to adjust so I suggest experimenting with it to find a position you like. I start the parallel weave by grasping the black Velour in my left hand and the orange with my right, never let the material leave the hand holding it during the weaving process. I'm going to refer to my hands as orange (right) and black (left). I'll bring the orange toward me and cross the black over the top of the shank.

Step 4: Now the orange moves forward then under the hook shank. I end this part of the step with the orange pointing to the left (held by the right hand) and the black to the right (held in position by the left hand). Note: Keeping the two colors of Velour (or chenille) in the same hand is what I learned at my first FFF Conclave. Before that I tried to accomplish the parallel weave switching the material from hand to hand. If you want an exercise in frustration give that method a try!

Step 5: Bring the black over the top of the hook shank so it points to the left. Bring the orange over the black, under the hook, and then straight to the left.

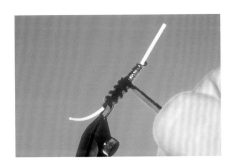

Step 6: Again, bring the black over the top so it points to the left. Bring the orange over the black, under the hook, and straight to the right. Repeat this process until the back half of the hook is covered. End with the orange under the hook and the black over the hook both facing the right with the black in front of the orange.

Step 7: Tilt the head back down and rotate the jaws one-quarter turn to return the vise to the normal-tying position. Retrieve the bobbin, tie the thread back on the shank at the center of the hook, and clip off the waste end. Tie both strands of Velour off on the near side of the hook. Do not trim off the excess Velour yet.

Step 8: Prepare a brown saddle feather by stripping the fuzzy material near the base of the stem. Tie it to the center of the hook shank. Bind the stem to the shank while advancing the thread to the front of the hook. Wrap the orange Velour forward, tie it off, and trim the waste end. This is an "either or" step. If you are not weighting the nymph then this extra layer of Velour is needed to build up bulk in the thorax area. On the hand, if you decide to wrap non-lead wire over this area the extra layer of Velour may not be needed. The fly tier must make that determination.

Step 9: Wrap the black Velour forward forming the thorax of the fly. Tie it off and trim the waste end. If any of the orange Velour shows through the black a felt tipped marker can easily make it disappear.

Step 10: Palmer the hackle over the thorax ending at the hook eye. Tie it off, trim the excess feather, whip-finish the thread, and trim it from the hook. I like to finish the fly with a coating of Aqua Head to seal the whip-finish. Be sure to separate the rubber leg material forming the tail and antenna. Did you remember to rotate the vise when applying the thorax and hackle? Just testing! Remember, this is a rotary tying book.

Green Belly Rat

Several years ago Gretchen and I were working on an order of steelhead flies for a customer in Washington. Among other patterns he had requested several Green Butt Skunks, a few woven-body Harvesters, and a couple of different flies from the Rat family. At the end of the order Gretchen went to the office to enter the invoice in the computer and I was supposed to package the flies. Before slipping them into their shipping container I decided to send along a couple of "joke" flies. What you see in the next several steps was the pattern I assembled for that purpose. It was not intended to catch fish, all I expected from it was a smile or two. I finished boxing the flies and mailed them without another thought; joke patterns were something I often included with orders. I promptly forgot about the fly as new orders came and went out the door to their respective customers.

As it turned out though, the joke was on me. About a month later the same customer called me requesting several dozen of the "special" flies I included with the last order. To save my life, I couldn't remember what pattern I sent him. Thankfully he still had one of the flies though it had been severely chewed by several fish. I asked him to send it to me as a sample. It arrived in the mail several days later, I completed the order, gave the fly a name, and entered it in my database for future reference.

I had to refer to the database quite often because my customer's friends decided it was a "must have" fly. Over the next several years Gretchen and I sent out a good number of that crazy pattern. At that time we lived in a part of the world where steelhead fishing was not an option. For about ten years we never used the fly. Then we moved back home to Idaho where steelhead fishing once again became one of our many angling opportunities.

Not long after the move we figured it was time to test drive the ole Green Belly ourselves and the gin clear water of the Salmon River near Stanley, Idaho was the selected location. On this water (unlike the Clearwater River in central Idaho) you can sight fish to steelhead holding in a lie within easy casting distance. We checked several runs until we found one where fish were holding. I eased into position and made my cast upstream so the fly could sink to the fish's level by the time the pattern reached the strike zone. I was sure success was within my grasp. The fish saw the fly and moved AWAY from it! Three more times I tried to entice the fish to take my offering, three more times it moved away from the fly. Throughout the afternoon I offered the Green Belly to several more fish and they either ignored or moved away from it. To save the day I finally switched to a Green Butt Skunk tied Spey style and I did hook a fish.

I've not had a lot of time to test this pattern more but as of this writing it has not touched a single fish for either Gretchen or me. Why did if work for my customer and his friends? I certainly don't know. I present it here with the hope that some of you will give it a try and let me know if it works for you. The main reason I selected it for this spot in the book is because it illustrates the overhand weave really well and again the latitude in adjusting the Mongoose vise makes that process much easier.

Green Belly Rat

Hook:	Size 2 to 8, steelhead
Thread:	Black
Body:	Brazilian Velour, black and green
Wing:	Gray squirrel tail
Hackle:	Black, tied as a collar

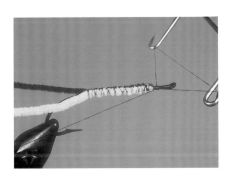

Step 1: Place the hook in the vise and apply a thread base that covers the shank ending at the looped eye platform. Select a black strand of Brazilian Velour and a green strand of the same material. Tie the green to the near side of the hook and the black to the off side. Trim any waste ends, whip-finish the thread, and clip it temporarily from the hook.

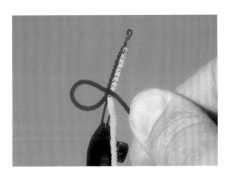

Step 2: Rotate the jaws one-quarter turn then tilt the complete vise head up so the hook is at a slight angle. Throughout the weaving process be sure to keep the black Velour on top and the green on the underside of the hook shank. Loop the black Velour over the top of the shank making certain it is slightly in front of the green. The black loop is on the off side of the hook (left of the photograph).

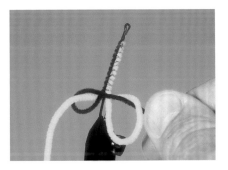

Step 3: Bring the green over the black Velour, under the hook shank, and through the black loop located on the off side of the hook.

Step 4: I like to adjust the black and green loops so they are similar in size. Pull on the loose ends of both strands of Velour to tighten the overhand knot.

Chapter 10: Griffin Enterprises, Inc.

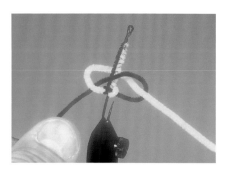

Step 5: Form a loop in the black Velour on the near side of the hook (right of the photograph) and lay it over the top of the shank. Bring the green Velour over the black, under the shank, and through the loop. Pull the knot tight.

Step 6: Repeat the process outlined in Steps 2 through 5 until the hook shank is covered. Be sure to leave room at the front for a wing and hackle. Tie the thread back on the hook and trim the waste end. Tie off both strands of Velour then trim them from the hook.

Step 7: Select a clump of gray squirrel tail fibers and tie it to the shank to form a wing that extends slightly past the hook bend. Trim the waste ends. Before I cover wrap the trimmed ends I like to apply a drop of crazy glue to further anchor the wing in position. Wrap over the trimmed ends. Select a black feather and fold the fibers in preparation for a wet-style collar application. Tie the feather on the hook in front of the wing by the feather's tip. I like to fold the tip over and again bind it to the hook to keep it from pulling out when I wrap the collar. I usually don't bother trimming off the tip because it just ends up hiding in the collar.

Step 8: Wrap the hackle collar by rotating the vise, tie off the feather, and trim away the waste end. Whip-finish the thread and trim it from the hook. I like to add a coating of Aqua Flex to complete the fly.

Allan Schultz founded Peak Engineering & Automation Company in 1994 and a year later Kurt Flock joined the organization. Both were avid fly-fishers but didn't tie flies. In 2000 they attended a fly-tying class with fellow employee Robert Kofron taught by another engineer friend of theirs, Al Ritt. They really enjoyed Al's instruction but being the analytical engineer types found the classroom vises somewhat lacking in quality.

Upon completing the class the trio decided they could make a better vise and keep the price tag under $200.00. The Peak Rotary Vise really hits the

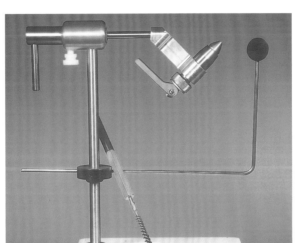

The Peak Vise and the Ritt Pick-N-Brush are two superb tools from the Peak Engineering & Automation Company.

mark and is the first fully machined, all-steel piece of equipment in its price range. The pedestal holds the vise rock solid and the workmanship is excellent. The rotating arm is constructed from stainless steel and the rotary turret is turned from a solid piece of brass. A delrin friction screw allows rotation adjustment from free spinning to a fixed position and is conveniently located adjacent to the rotating handle. The standard jaw holds a range of hook sizes from 2/0 to 24. Saltwater and midge jaws are available for the tier who regularly tie flies into the extreme of mid-range sizes. I especially liked the bobbin rest. It provides solid support while remaining easy to move out of the way when not required.

Another item by Peak I really enjoyed is their Ritt Pick-N-Brush illustrated here with the vise. It has a bodkin on one end and a nylon bristled brush on the other for teasing out dubbing without cutting thread. Oh yeah. They thoughtfully included a cap to protect the point; actually it's supposed to protect me from the needle.

The Peak Vise is simple, rugged, and manufactured right here in the good, old USA in Loveland, Colorado. Its attractive price is well under the $200.00 mark.

Spruce Fly Streamer

I love to fish streamer patterns and consider myself quite good at it. I've always liked bucktail streamers because they have a good profile while also providing the illusion of dimension like a natural baitfish presents. Unfortunately they don't have the same action other materials like feathers or marabou bring to a sub-surface pattern. Fortunately the bucktail doesn't foul around the hook like some of the items I just mentioned. I pondered the problem (stiffer wings or action materials that fouled the hook) for the better part of ten years. I even tried wrapping a marabou feather around a clump of bucktail. Boy, what a disaster!

The answer came to me in the mid 90s from a couple of different directions. I'm not sure where I stumbled on the method I now use for tying a peacock-body Elk Hair Caddis. In it the hackle, peacock, and thread are all mixed/spun together (see this book, Chapter Six). One day when I was replenishing my EHC box I realized the hackle around the peacock/thread center was just the profile I needed on my feather-wing streamers. I knew if I could capture that profile, using streamer-sized feathers, I would have the dimension to my feather-wing streamers I wanted.

The answer didn't come easy. I tried putting glue on my thread, winding the hackle around it, and allowing it to dry. The resulting streamer looked great but only lasted a few minutes under normal fishing conditions. I put the idea temporarily on a "back burner." The answer came from an unexpected person, Jon Strand from Oslo, Norway.

One summer Jon and a couple of his friends came to visit Gretchen and me in our Bozeman, Montana home. They fished hard all day then tied flies half the night. I don't know when those young men ever slept but they managed to slip it in somewhere. One evening I joined them in the tying room for a few minutes. They were tying stonefly nymphs using a new product out of the Czech Republic called a Dubbing Brush. It was fur placed in a wire loop spun to look like a piece of chenille with a twisted wire core. For me the idea light-bulb went off with a bang! A few minutes later I tied my first wire wings and put them on a streamer. It was the fly you will see here in a few minutes, a Spruce Fly Streamer (WW). As soon as I saw it I was sure I had a wing with built-in action that wouldn't foul around the hook.

Over the next couple of evenings I tied every kind of wire-wing streamer I could imagine. I even tie a few that incorporated Sili-Con Leg Material in them. A few days later I wasn't scheduled to guide so I took Gretchen fishing on the Yellowstone River. We floated one of my favorite sections, the bird run from Gray Owl to Mallard's Rest. Gretchen and I have long had this agreement; I row for her until she catches three fish then she rows for me until I catch my three. To cut a long story short, we both had a great day using those wire-wing streamers.

Late in the afternoon it clouded over and our fishing success came to a screeching halt. We anchored the drift boat in a back eddy just upstream from Mallard's Rest fishing access, took up a station in a large riffle, and ran a couple of wire wings through it. I switched patterns a couple of times with no change in the results; zero fish. I finally tied on one the patterns with Sili-Con material anchored to the end of the wire wing. I dropped the pattern in the moving water at my feet; it sure looked wild with the rubber leg material flopping around in the current. I made a cast slightly upstream from my station, threw a couple of stack mends, and was hard into a good fish before the fly had drifted ten feet. I gave Gretchen the other Sili-Con wire wing (I only had two with me) and we enjoyed another hour of great fishing.

About a half hour before dark I lost my fly on a rock and decided to call it a day. I told Gretchen I would take the boat to the landing, load it on the trailer, and drive to the upstream end of the fishing access to pick her up; she would only have a hundred-yard walk at most. When I got to the pickup location, she wasn't there. So I grabbed a flashlight and went looking for her. There she was with her rod bent almost in two, fighting a really good fish. A few minutes later she lost it (and the fly) and we headed for home, two very happy fly-fishers. The next day I was back on the river with customers and Gretchen tied wire-wing flies; many of them had Sili-Con at the end of the wings.

We still fish a lot of wire-wing flies but for some reason the only place we had success with Sili-Con material at the end of the wings was in Montana. When we moved to Colorado those crazy wings literally scared the fish into hiding. The same thing happened here in Idaho; the fish seem to be put off by the Sili-Con addition to the wings. However, they like the wire wing flies just fine. I have not tried the Sili-Con version on Idaho's bass yet but will very soon.

Spruce Fly Streamer

Hook:	Size 4 to 10, streamer
Thread:	Black
Tail:	Peacock herl
Body:	Red floss, peacock herl
Wings:	Brown or furnace hackle, red wire
Hackle:	Brown or furnace, as a collar
Head:	Thread

Step 1: Let's start by constructing the wire wing. Place a hook in the vise and attach the tying thread behind the eye. Select two or four neck feathers all about the same size. Place them so they oppose each other (single or in pairs) and tie them temporarily to the hook by the base of the stem with the tips pointing forward. Select a length of red wire (about 26 or 28 gage) twice as long as the wing and tie one end on top of the feathers with the long end pointing forward. Pull the feathers and wire together then anchor them in an EZY grip hackle pliers or electronics test clip near the tips of the feathers. Hold the assembly straight out in front of the vise.

Step 2: Stroke the fibers on the hackle back so they stick out from the stems. Take the loose end of the wire and loop it around the feathers with the wire core tight against the hackle pliers. Pull the loose end back to the hook and anchor it on top of the other end of the wire/feathers.

Step 3: Rotate the vise several turns to twist the wire and feathers into a single assembly. The tighter you twist the wire the fuller/shorter the wing will be. Don't twist the wire too tight or it will break.

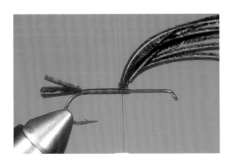

Step 4: Cut the wire-wing assembly from the hook. Don't use your best pair of scissors if you want to keep them sharp. Set the wing aside for the moment. Lay down a thread base that covers the back half of the hook starting and stopping in the center of the shank. Select several peacock herls and tie them to the shank to form a tail as long as the hook gape. Tie on a segment of red floss and wrap it over the back half of the hook. Tie it off and trim any waste ends.

Step 5: Grasp the peacock herl/thread and pull them straight in front of the vise. Rotate the vise several turns to form peacock chenille around a thread core.

Step 6: Bring the chenille perpendicular to the hook shank and rotate the vise again to apply the front part of the body. Tie off the herls and trim the excess from the hook.

Step 7: Retrieve the wing set aside in Step 4 and tie it to the hook. I like the wings to extend behind the hook equal to one-half of the hook shank. With the wire core there is certainly no problem with a wing fouled around the hook bend. Trim the waste end using an old pair of scissors. It really makes no difference but I like to position the wing so the little feather tips at the end point up.

Step 8: Fold a hackle and tie it to the shank by the tip. Rotate the vise to wind a collar, tie it off, and trim the waste end of the feather. Apply a whip-finish, tie off the thread, and trim it from the hook. Complete the fly with a coat of Aqua Flex to seal the windings in the whip-finish.

Dave's Emerger

It sure is interesting how life works out sometimes. I just put this bit of information together after speaking with the fly's originator, Dave Corcoran from Bozeman, Montana. It really is two stories that just came together for me.

All through the 80s I worked as a manager for a large utility company in Sandpoint, Idaho located just thirty miles from the Montana border. Most weekends/holidays found me fishing using my drift boat on the Clark Fork River upstream from Saint Regis, Montana. I was lucky enough to enjoy that river when often my boat was the only one I would see during a day on the water. Often friends would join me with the agreement they would take their turn on the oars. Sometimes that expectation actually worked out and other times I spent most of the day rowing. I learned to select fishing companions carefully and weed out those who couldn't learn the art of the oars.

In the spring of '87 I met Bob Lay at a utilities convention. During a conversation over dinner one evening I learned he was a fly-fisher and lived/worked in Kalispell, Montana, a three-hour drive from my home. It didn't take us long to figure out the Clark Fork River would be a great place to meet for a weekend of fly-fishing. The very next weekend we met at a little restaurant in Plans, Montana and after breakfast Bob insisted on taking the oars first thing in the morning. He stayed on them until early afternoon when it was my turn. By the time we made the switch a great friendship was in the making and Bob was well on his way to becoming a darned good oarsman. Before the weekend passed and it was time to return to work we had decided to spend time on the Bighorn River the second week in September.

The Bighorn turned out to be everything we had heard it could be. We met a couple of Bozeman guides at dinner one evening and as often happens when fly-fishers get together our conversation turned to the day's successful flies. That was the first time I ever saw a Dave's Emerger. Little did I know that in a few years I would see many more than I ever imagined.

During the mid 80s Dave Corcoran (then owner of the River's Edge Fly Shop) would often be at the Bighorn for a couple of months at a time staying at the Lariat Motel in Hardin, Montana. Anyone who has spent time in that town knows there is not much to do. Designing flies was a good way to pass the hours not spent on the water and the river itself was a great test area for any new patterns. His emerger was a cross between a Brassy, a Pheasant Tail Nymph, and a Light Cahill wet fly. Dave liked to apply fly floatant to the wing and fish it in the surface film rather than on top of the water. The fish liked the fly and Dave's Emerger was an instant success.

When Gretchen and I moved to Bozeman to start our new life tying flies and guiding Dave gave us our first fly order. Can you guess what pattern it was? Yup! It was an order for fifty dozen Dave's Emerger flies. Over the next several years we tied hundreds of dozens of that pattern with either a copper body or one constructed from red wire.

During our second year in Bozeman Dave asked me to guide for him and I really learned how well his Emerger attracted fish. My start-the-day rig was a Royal Wulff with a Bead Head Prince Nymph on a dropper for one client and a Parachute Hopper with a Dave's Emerger for the other. One or all of the flies in that combination usually brought a fish to the boat. Often the Dave's Emerger accounted for the first and the most fish.

Not only is the fly attractive to fish but its construction also lends well to rotary tying techniques. You will soon see how easy it is to construct a copper wire body using a rotating vise.

Dave's Emerger

Hook:	Size 12 to 20, dry fly
Thread:	Rusty brown
Tail:	Woodduck fibers
Abdomen:	Copper or red wire
Thorax:	Peacock herl
Wing case:	Woodduck fibers
Wing:	Woodduck fibers
Head:	Thread or optional copper bead

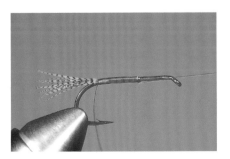

Step 1: Place a hook in the vise and lay down a thread base that covers the front one-half of the shank. Trim off the waste end of thread and leave the bobbin hanging in the center of the hook. Select a sparse clump of woodduck fibers and tie them on the shank forming a tail as long as the width of the hook gape. Tie on a six-inch segment of copper wire while advancing the thread back to the center of the hook. Apply a half hitch then place the thread in the bobbin cradle. Trim off the waste ends of feather and wire.

Chapter 11: Peak Vise

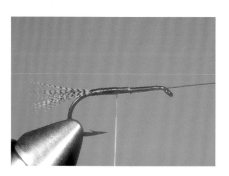

Step 2: Rotate the vise to apply the wire body. If I hold the wire slightly toward the rear of the hook I can get a very smooth, even application. The wire need only be about one degree off perpendicular to force each turn tight against the previous.

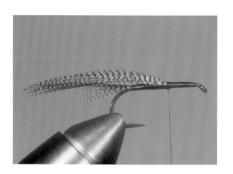

Step 3: Finish wrapping the body, tie off the wire, and trim the waste end. Select a clump of woodduck fibers that are equal in length to the shank and tail. Tie the bundle to the hook with the tips pointing to the rear. Trim off any excess material. Notice I positioned the feather so the natural curve faced down. Leave the thread in the center of the hook.

Step 4: Select several peacock herls and tie them to the hook by their tips. Pull the herl/thread out in front of the hook and rotate the vise to construct a strand of peacock chenille. Bring the chenille perpendicular to the shank then rotate the vise to apply the thorax. Tie off the herl and trim away any waste ends. Be careful to avoid crowding the hook eye.

Step 5: Pull the woodduck fibers placed in Step 3 over to form a wing case. Bind them to the hook with several thread wraps. Do not trim off the tips; instead pull them back to form a Trude-style wing. Form a head, apply a whip-finish, and trim the thread from the hook. Sometimes one of the fibers doesn't want to lay right so I'll use my scissors to correct the problem.

Step 6: I like to place a drop of Aqua Tuff to complete the fly. The Ritt Pick-N-Brush works really well for that job.

Buzz Ball

This is a Gary LaFontaine pattern developed to imitate a clump of adult midges. Quite frankly I had never used the fly until Gretchen and I, along with Paul and Char Stimpson, started working with Gary on a series of videos chronicling his patterns. Of course the Buzz Ball was among them. As we worked on scripting for the videos he kept bringing up the fly. He felt it was one of his most effective patterns, especially when used in an environment with midges; a very common bug on many western waters. When we did the video shoot we ended up with a couple of the flies so I just tossed them in the box where I kept my Griffith's Gnats.

The two flies stayed there for the better part of a year. Gretchen and I didn't get a chance to do much fishing during that time frame because we were busy moving from Colorado back to her hometown in Idaho. After getting settled in Boise we attended a meeting of a local fly-fishing club. The president, Jeff Smith, offered to take us fishing on one of the local streams and we gladly accepted.

It turned out to be a river with a huge population of midges. Our first day on the water was cloudy with adult midges hatching profusely and the trout feeding aggressively. I caught a few fish on a Griffith's Gnat but wouldn't say it was THE hot pattern. I even tried my never-fails-me, always-go-to Renegade and it didn't provide the results I expected. Finally in desperation I tied on one of the Buzz Balls and hooked up on the first cast. From that point the day changed from just so-so to great until I lost both flies to really big fish.

That evening when we got home Gretchen and I tied several dozen in sizes twelve to sixteen. The next day on the river was memorable until the sun broke through the clouds and the midge hatch stopped like we had turned off a faucet. Today our midge boxes have a few Griffith's Gnats and a whole bunch of Buzz Balls. I like the body with a little less orange in it than Gary suggested in his original recipe. I prefer the trimmed part of the body be about two-thirds dun and one-third orange. You can experiment to find what works best on your waters but whatever you do I highly recommend several of these flies be included in your assortment of midge patterns. Gary also tied an "improved" version of the fly by adding a short Antron spike at the front to provide better visibility to the angler. It's your choice which version you choose to tie. I like the standard Buzz Ball so that's what I'm demonstrating here.

Buzz Ball

Hook:	Size 10 to 16, dry fly
Thread:	Black or gray
Body:	Two dun and one orange hackle feathers, trimmed
Hackle:	Grizzly, palmered and trimmed top & bottom
Spike:	Optional Antron tuft
Head:	Thread

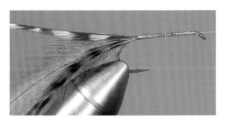

Step 1: Place the hook in the vise, attach the tying thread just behind the eye, and wrap it to the end of the shank. Prepare a grizzly, two medium dun, and a grizzly-dyed orange hackle feathers by stripping the fuzzy material from the base of the stems. Place the two dun and the orange feathers on top of the grizzly and tie all of them to the shank while wrapping the thread forward to meet the hook eye. Place the thread in a bobbin rest and the grizzly feather in a materials keeper.

Step 2: Grasp the two dun and the single orange feathers with the right hand and use the left to rotate the vise. Turn the vise as many rotations as it takes to reach the front of the hook. Tie off the three feathers and trim away the excess. I like to store the extra feathers in a clothespin in preparation for the next fly.

Step 3: Rotate the vise one-half turn and clip the bottom from the body. Rotate the vise a partial turn and again trim the body. Continue this process until all of the hackle in the body has been trimmed to length. I suggest placing the thread in the bobbin rest prior to starting this process.

Step 4: Remove the grizzly hackle from the materials keeper, hold it with the right hand, and rotate the vise with the left to palmer the hackle over the newly trimmed body.

Step 5: Tie off the grizzly feather and clip the excess from the hook. Rotate the vise one-half turn and trim the bottom of the grizzly hackle even with the body. Rotate the vise another half turn and repeat the process on the top of the fly.

Step 6: Add the optional Antron spike if you want to tie the "improved" version. Apply a whip-finish, trim the thread from the hook, and place a drop of Aqua Tuff to finish the fly.

Marts Down-eye Carp Fly

Gretchen and my fishing flies come from many different sources. I would like to say they are all a result of our own creativity but that would just be a case of my ego getting in the way of reality. Our fly boxes are full of other people's ideas with a few patterns modified just a bit to give us a sense of a personal touch. Other patterns went in the box with no modification at all. That's the case with this pattern.

We got this fly from Bill Marts owner of the Blue Dun Fly Shop in Spokane, Washington. He called one day last winter to place an order. After identifying the items he needed our conversation turned to other topics as they often did. Business stats, inventory turns, what's

selling, what's not, and carp fishing. Carp fishing! Yes, I have to admit I'm a closet carp fisher and Bill Marts is about as close as I have to a mentor on the subject. He is a well-recognized expert carp fisher and quite frankly I'm still struggling with it. I catch a few carp on a fly but I really think is more of an accident than any special skills I have.

I asked Bill if he had any new patterns or techniques he would share. He told me he had started fishing for carp with his Spey rod. He really sucked me in on that one. I bit and asked the question, "So, how do you do that?" His response was one word, "Dapping." I was stunned but soon recovered enough to ask questions like, "How? Flies? Where?" He answered all of my questions and promised to send me several samples of his dapping flies. They arrived several days later and what I'm sharing with you today is one of those patterns.

I'd like to say Bill's dapping flies solved all my carp fishing problems but that just wouldn't be true. Yes, in some situations dapping for carp is a very productive technique but about the time I get to thinking I have it "dialed in" I get skunked and realize those darned carp were just playing with me all along. I think skill and experience is part of the reason Bill is such a well-rounded angler. I guess that's why I'm the student and he's the mentor. Anyway this fly is really easy to tie using rotary techniques so let's get to it.

Marts Down-eye Carp

Hook:	Size 2 to 8, nymph
Thread:	Rusty brown
Weight:	Dumbbell eyes
Body:	Brown sparkle chenille
Hackle:	Grizzly, palmered
Head:	Thread

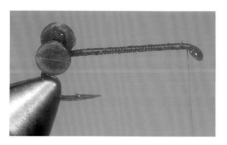

Step 1: Mount the hook in the vise and lay down a thread base that covers the complete hook shank. Bind a set of dumbbell eyes at the start of the hook bend with several tight, crisscross thread wraps. I like to follow with a drop of crazy glue to further anchor them in place. Leave the thread hanging near the hook eye.

Step 2: Select a length of chenille and bind it to the top of the hook. Wrap a single criss-cross wrap of chenille around the eyes and tie it to the shank in front of them. Do not trim it.

Step 3: Select a grizzly saddle feather and strip the fuzzy material from the base of the stem. Tie it to the shank in front of the eyes. Rotate the vise to apply chenille. Remember whenever advancing a materials with thread, the thread leads the process. Tie off the chenille body and trim away the waste end.

Step 4: Rotate the vise to palmer the hackle over the body. Tie it off and trim the waste end. Construct a whip-finish and clip the thread from the hook. Apply a coating of Aqua Head to complete the fly.

Renzetti Vises

Andy Renzetti first introduced the Bent Shaft Vise design in 1979. Since then it has become recognized worldwide. Gretchen and I attend fly-tying shows all over the world and we've never attended one where there was not at least a half dozen in use by non-American fly-dressers. That tells me Andy has a quality tool and a great distribution network. In fact, in reviewing his web site, he has a lot of quality vises, tools, and accessories.

The Bent Shaft design is quite unique. So much so that last December the United States Trademark and Patent office granted Renzetti Inc. a Trade Dress registration giving the company the exclusive right to the use of the bent-shaft design. The Master (pictured here) is the only vise in Renzetti's product line that does not have the bent-arm design. It is designed so the jaw can swing up and down to allow the shank on a wide range of hooks to remain on "axis." The jaw closing mechanism is easily accessible by either right- or left-handed fly tiers. Some of the other vises in the Renzetti product line must be ordered specifying whether the tier is right or left handed.

Andy identifies the Master as a vise that will hold hooks from size 28 to 10/0 while some of his other vises aren't designed to handle hooks quite that big. I have to admit I've never tied a 10/0 fly but the Master you see here has held several 9/0 hooks with no problem. It also has the traditional rotary actuator that allows the tier to rotate the jaws by turning the rotary arm. I really like the movable materials keeper, it's easy to swing in position when you need it and or push it down out of the way if you don't.

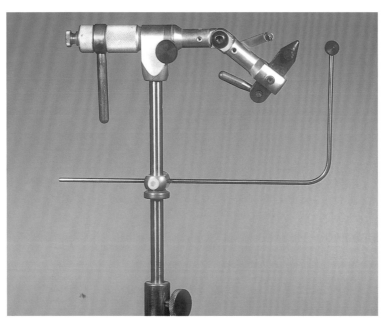

I really like the movable materials keeper on this Renzetti vise.

The Bunny Leech

I guess the old saying "out of sight, out of mind" would fit how this fly wormed its way in and out of our lives. During our Montana years, the contents of our fly boxes were never without an assortment of Bunny Leeches. The black, olive, and white were my personal favorites but I always included one or two flies in other colors. They served me well on the Yellowstone and Madison rivers, especially when I was fishing from a drift boat "pounding the banks." Yes, I often think of crisp, fall days while floating the Yellowstone River. The cottonwood trees were a light golden color and the brown trout were down-right savage. I always found it kind of ironic; the same fish that were so shy in August became like marauding Mongolian horsemen in October. Bunny flies were my pattern of choice.

Then we moved to Delta, Colorado where I went to work for Whiting Farms as their marketing director. One of the advantages of being a "feather junky" (and being married to one as well) was access to every possible exotic plumage imaginable. Part of my job was testing the many feathers Tom Whiting was selling or planned to offer the market in the future. As a result those feathers gradually took control of our fly boxes, kicking the bunny patterns out in the process. I refer you to my comment in the previous chapter about being out of sight and out of mind. I didn't realize it but I didn't fish bunny flies for about three years.

The last year we were in Delta was the year we spent writing/editing the *Fly Pattern Encyclopedia*. One day I was opening packages from fly tiers and entering their flies in the appropriate section of the book. As I worked my way through the stack of boxes I came to one from Mel Krieger. Upon opening it I found a white Bunny Leech inside with a nice note from him. I asked Gretchen, "Did you know Mel Krieger tied flies?" She answered, "No, I didn't." I had the evidence in my hand and any of you interested will find Mel's fly in that book on page 144.

Mel's Bunny Leech reminded me we had not fished such a fly in a heck of a long time. After finishing my writing for the day I tied a couple dozen Bunny Leeches and they have not been AWOL from my fly boxes since!

When I started fishing bunny flies I was frustrated with their tendency to foul around the hook bend. While living in Montana I found a solution to that problem and I'll share it with you in the next few minutes.

Bunny Leech

Hook:	Size 2/0 to 8, streamer
Thread:	Black
Tail support:	Extended monofilament loop
Tail:	Chartreuse bunny strip or color of choice
Body:	Black bunny strip or color of choice
Head:	Thread

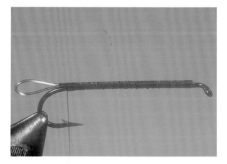

Step 1: Place the hook in the vise and apply a thread base from the hook eye to the end of the shank. Fold a six-inch segment of thirty-pound monofilament in half and tie it to the top of the shank. I find it easier to apply if I start at the back of the hook and wrap forward binding the monofilament as I go. Trim the waste ends and wrap the thread to the back of the hook. I like to take six or eight thread wraps around the monofilament loop where it extends beyond the shank. Leave the thread at the back of the hook in preparation for the next step.

Step 2: Select a section of straight-cut rabbit strip and tie it to the end of the shank. Use a razor blade to cut the hide forming a tail with a length determined by the tier. I like mine about as long as the hook shank. I'm using a crosscut rabbit strip in the next step to form the body. Notice the hair sticks out to the side on the black crosscut strip and the fur is straight on the chartreuse tail. In the water it makes no difference which type of strip you use but I like the way the fly looks in the photograph when it's constructed from the two types of rabbit strip.

Step 3: Tie the black crosscut strip to the end of the shank with the fibers facing back. Wrap the thread forward and place it in the bobbin rest. Apply the body by grasping the rabbit strip with the right hand and use the left to rotate the vise. Turn the vise as many times as it takes to cover the hook shank. Remove the thread from the bobbin rest and tie off the rabbit strip.

Step 4: Clip the rabbit strip from the hook and wrap a thread head. Apply a whip-finish and trim the thread from the hook. In the water this fly presents a slender, undulating profile with a chartreuse hot spot at the very end of the pattern. If you haven't figured it out by now, I like hot spots built into most my flies. I guess Gary LaFontaine was a pretty strong influence in my fishing beliefs. You'll have to decide if it was good or not or better yet give the hot-spot theory a try for yourself.

Harvester

During our last year working in corporate America Gretchen was stationed in Silver Lake, Washington and I was a two-hour drive away on the other side of the Cascade Mountains in Wenatchee. Our regular work week was long and lonesome; the weekends were too darned short. On some weekends I would drive to Silver Lake to see Gretchen and on others she would come to Wenatchee.

On one such weekend I told her I had a special surprise. That evening we attended the banquet/fund-raiser for the local club, the Wenatchee Valley Fly Fishers. I already knew many of the members from attending their club meetings and monthly fly-tying clinics but for Gretchen it was a night of many introductions. We had the good fortune to sit with Bill and Judy Marts, co-owners of the Blue Dun Fly Shop.

As the evening unfolded dinner melted into the live auction and Bill Marts was our auctioneer. Gretchen and I have been to many auctions and it quickly became very evident that Bill Marts was a master in the art of extracting money from people's wallets, mine included.

Toward the end of the evening I noticed a box of three steelhead flies tied by our auctioneer was the last item on the list. When the bidding opened I noticed a sudden change in the crowd as several very skilled fly-fishers jumped into the fray. "I wonder what they know that we don't?" I commented to Gretchen as the bidding shot through the roof. She didn't know but I decided I better have those Harvester flies myself. I finally got them but I'll be darned if I tell all of you how much I paid for them. Suffice to say, it was a lot more than I should have!

On the way home that evening we talked about the fun we had and the great new friends we met. Gretchen told me she had talked with Bill about tying several commercial orders for the Blue Dun to help pass the long evenings alone in Silver Lake. I thought it was a great idea; I was already doing the same myself.

The next day we stopped in at the Blue Dun and Bill gave Gretchen an order for twenty-five dozen Harvesters.

We asked Bill how he wanted them tied and he explained a dry-fly hackle wrapped behind the marabou made it pulse in water without completely collapsing in the current. We left the shop knowing Gretchen would be busy for the next few weeks and we had the secret to Bill's hot steelhead fly. Now all of you will know as well! I am going to tie my version of the Harvester that is quite successful on steelhead here in Idaho.

Harvester

Hook:	Size 2/0 to 8, salmon
Thread:	Chartreuse
Tag:	Chartreuse floss
Ribs:	Oval silver tinsel, two
Body:	Black yarn
Under hackle:	Black dry fly
Hackle collar:	Black and chartreuse marabou
Collar front:	Natural guinea
Head:	Thread

Step 1: With the hook mounted in the vise, lay down a thread base from the eye loop to a position directly above the point. Select a six-inch piece of chartreuse floss. Tie it on the hook, wrap it down into the bend, and back to the starting point. Tie it off and trim any waste ends. Cut two segments of silver oval tinsel from a spool and bind both of them to the bottom of the hook while advancing the thread back to the eye.

Step 2: Select an eight-inch section of black four-strand yarn and remove one of the segments. Tie it to the top of the shank while wrapping the thread back to meet the tag. Hold the thread and yarn with the right hand and rotate the vise to wrap the body. I find I get a smooth application of yarn if I twist it until I see the strands align themselves.

Step 3: Tie off the yarn and trim it from the hook. Place a half hitch in the thread and position it over the bobbin rest. Grasp one of the strands of tinsel and rotate the vise to apply the first rib.

Step 4: Tie it off, place a half hitch, and return the thread to the bobbin rest. Grasp the second rib and rotate the vise in the *opposite* direction to cross the tinsel over the first application. Tie it off and trim away the waste end of each rib.

Chapter 12: Renzetti Vises

Step 5: Prepare a black saddle feather by stripping the fuzzy material from the base of the stem. Tie it on the hook and place the thread in the bobbin rest. Grasp the feather and rotate the vise to place six turns of hackle each directly *behind* each other. Continue rotating the vise and place six more turns of hackle with each in *front* of the previous turn. Tie off the hackle and trim away the waste end. Doubling the hackle in this manner provides a firm base behind the marabou collar to stop it from collapsing while subsurface under tension from the angler. Also, I like the hackle to be two sizes smaller than the hook in the vise; in this case I placed a size-six hackle on a number-two hook.

Step 6: Remove the fibers from the base of the stem of a chartreuse marabou feather. Tie it on the hook and wrap a three-turn application. Anchor the tip to the hook and trim off the waste end.

Step 7: Repeat the process with a black marabou feather.

Step 8: Prepare and wrap a natural guinea feather front to the collar. Tie it off and trim the waste end. I like to complete the fly with a coating of Aqua Flex or Aqua Tuff over the thread head. Dry the fly in a turning wheel to be certain the glue dries evenly.

Bead Belly Zonker

I've been looking forward to the last two flies because I really wanted to share with you a discovery I made in winter 2003. I met Steve Duckett at the International Sportsmen's Exposition in San Mateo, California. He asked me to look over a fly he had developed. I was busy working my booth and I was alone so promised to look it over at my motel that evening after the show.

That night I opened his package with a little trepidation. I often receive flies people have developed only to see a pattern almost exactly like the... I'll let you fill in the blank. Over the years I have seldom seen anything really revolutionary. I expected the same as I opened Steve's package. What I saw was a real surprise!

He had taken standard patterns and added a monofilament loop to the belly with beads on it to act as ballast. The beads flip the fly over so it travels through the water column hook point up but they also function as a rattle. Steve calls them a "dinner bell" for the fish. Also, the natural curve of the monofilament loop slides the fly up and over many underwater obstructions. Check out some of Steve's creations at www.bouncerflies.com. I think you will be surprised.

I've not had the chance to test drive Steve's design but as soon as I get this book sent to the editors I'll be on my local waters fishing several of my standard streamer patterns with his modification. The Zonker tied like a sculpin has long been a favorite of mine. I'm not going into a long explanation why I like it, suffice it to say it looks like a sculpin and has a lot of action in the water. What I'm interested to learn is how the Bead Belly version attracts the fish. I'm going to tie my first right now. I'll have to share the fishing results with all of you at another time.

Bead Belly Zonker

Hook:	Size 2 to 10, streamer
Thread:	Black
Tail support:	Extended monofilament loop
Belly loop:	Monofilament
Body:	White yarn
Fins:	Soft hackle and chickabou tips
Tail & wing:	Rabbit strip
Gills:	Red dubbing
Collar:	Spun deer hair
Head:	Spun & trimmed deer hair
Weight:	Several beads

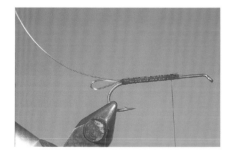

Step 1: Place the hook in the vise and apply a thread base that covers the back three-fourths of the shank. Fold a six-inch segment of thirty-pound monofilament in half and tie it to the top of the shank. Trim the waste ends and wrap the thread to the back of the hook. I like to take six or eight thread wraps around the monofilament loop where it extends beyond the shank. Select a short section of fifteen-pound monofilament and bind it on top of the loop over the back part of the hook. Leave the thread hanging at the one-quarter position.

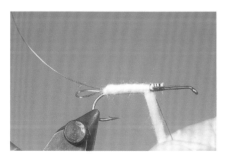

Step 2: Tie a section of white yarn on top of the hook stopping at the end of the shank. Grasp the thread/yarn with the right hand and rotate the vise to apply the body.

Step 3: Finish wrapping the body, tie off the yarn, and trim the waste end from the hook. From a soft hackle with chickabou patch, select two of each type of feather. On the off side of the hook tie on a soft hackle feather tip and top it with a short tuft of chickabou. Trim any waste ends. Repeat the process on the near side of the hook. I think the little tuft of chickabou gives an otherwise non-moving fin the illusion of life.

Step 4: Select a rabbit strip; I'm using rust colored because it is a fair match for the natural sculpins in my part of the world. Remove the hook from the vise and impale the strip over the point. Return the hook to the vise then rotate it one-half turn. From this point in time ALL references to *top* and *bottom* of the fly have changed. I'll give you a "heads up" if I change back.

Step 5: Pull the wing into position on top of the fly, measure it for length, and cut off the unneeded part of the strip. Bind the wing in place with several tight thread wraps. Apply red dubbing to the thread and wind it over those wraps. The dubbing covers the thread and provides the gills as well. Now is a good time to slip the tail through the monofilament loop placed in Step 1.

Step 6: Select, clean, and stack a clump of deer hair. Spin it around the hook to form the collar. Did you remember to rotate the vise to accomplish this application? Spin another clump or two of hair to form the head. Be sure to leave plenty of room near the hook eye to tie down the monofilament.

Step 7: Rotate the vise and trim the head/collar flat along the bottom of the pattern. Trim the rest of the head so it is flat and triangular in shape.

Step 8: Cut the monofilament loop to length and place the beads on it. On the illustrated fly I used three 3mm beads, two 4mm beads, and one 5mm bead placing the smallest near the back and the largest at the front. Melt a small ball on the end of the monofilament and tie it on the hook at the eye. The ball is needed to keep the slick monofilament from slipping out from under the thread wraps. Apply a whip-finish, trim the thread from the hook, and place a coat of Aqua Flex to complete the fly. I think this will be one hot pattern; time will tell.

Bucktail Bunny (BB)

I love to fly-fish for bass and pike. We have many opportunities to enjoy this aspect of our sport. There are several good bass waters close to my home in Boise and a number of lakes filled with pike in my old stopping grounds in north Idaho. When Mel Krieger inadvertently reminded me I had stopped fly-fishing with bunny patterns I got back into it big time with those warmwater species in mind.

This fly is bits and pieces from several patterns, a Clouser Minnow, a Bunny Leech, and a Zonker. I've caught a lot of fish on bunny flies because they look so alive in the water. I've fished this fly (the non-bead belly version) for the past couple of years since returning to Idaho and it's treated me very well. There are a couple of bass ponds not too far from my home whose residence are real suckers for it. Last month while outlining this chapter I was looking for a fourth fly having the first three pretty well established in my mind's eye, settling on the one you see here sans the bead belly. Then last night I awoke in bed thinking about Steve's bead-belly design and had to share it with all of you. It didn't take a lot of imagination to change the Zonker Sculpin and the Bucktail Bunny into bead-belly cousins to the original patterns. I can guarantee you when I finish this chapter and mail the manuscript to Frank Amato I'll be in the field giving them a thorough test drive. I'm as excited about the potential of the bead-belly design as I've been in a long time. Thanks to Steve Duckett's innovation.

Bucktail Bunny

Hook:	Size 3/0 to 2, bass/warmwater
Thread:	White
Tail:	White bucktail
Belly loop:	Monofilament
Body:	White rabbit strip
Wing:	Olive rabbit strip
Weight:	Beads
Head:	Thread, felt-tip marker
Eyes:	Stick-on, optional

Step 1: Mount the hook in the vise and apply a thread base that covers the back 7/8 of the shank. Select a clump of white bucktail and tie it to the shank forming a tail a little longer than the complete hook. Tie a six-inch section of fifteen-pound monofilament to later use as the belly loop.

Step 2: Tie a white rabbit strip on the hook at the end of the shank. Grasp the thread and material with the right hand and rotate the vise to apply the body. Tie off the rabbit strip and trim the waste end. Be careful not to crowd the hook eye.

Chapter 12: Renzetti Vises

Step 3: Select an olive rabbit strip, remove the hook from the vise, and impale the strip over the point. Return the hook to the vise then rotate it one-half turn so the hook point is up. Pull the rabbit strip tight over the body and anchor it at the front of the hook. Cut off the rabbit strip and wrap over the trimmed end.

Step 4: Slip several beads on the monofilament so there is enough weight to be sure the hook point rides up. I placed the larger beads to the front and the smaller to the back. Melt a small ball on the end of the monofilament and tie it to the hook at the eye.

Step 5: Wrap a smooth head, apply a whip finish, and trim the thread from the hook. Use a felt-tipped marker to color the head.

Step 6: Position the stick-on eyes and press them into place. Coat each with Aqua Flex as well as the head. Place the fly on a turning wheel to dry, then apply a second coat if it is needed.

Conclusion

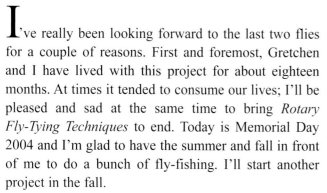

I've really been looking forward to the last two flies for a couple of reasons. First and foremost, Gretchen and I have lived with this project for about eighteen months. At times it tended to consume our lives; I'll be pleased and sad at the same time to bring *Rotary Fly-Tying Techniques* to end. Today is Memorial Day 2004 and I'm glad to have the summer and fall in front of me to do a bunch of fly-fishing. I'll start another project in the fall.

My other reason is sharing with all of you the bead-belly fly design outlined in the Chapter 12. It's going to be fun testing those patterns in our area waters and I have the whole summer to do it. By the time you read these pages that summer will be long past but know we both had a great time.

For Gretchen and me it was our goal to bring you techniques you may use to improve your tying and provide a better understanding of what a really great tool a true rotary vise can be. Until next time...

Farewell and Tight Lines
—Al & Gretchen Beatty
Boise, Idaho

Index